NORTH AMERICAN
WILDLIFE

NORTH AMERICAN WILDLIFE

George Laycock

with an Introduction by Isaac Asimov

NEW YORK

First published in USA 1983
by Exeter Books
Distributed by Bookthrift
Exeter is a trademark of Simon & Schuster
Bookthrift is a registered trademark of Simon & Schuster
New York, New York

ISBN 0-671-06005-8

Printed in Hong Kong

Above: A bighorn sheep in Glacier Nation Park.

Page 1: A whitetail deer in Tennessee.

Page 2-3: Bison in Yellowstone.

Contents

Natural Features of North America
Showing Major Mountains and Larger Canadian and American National Parks and Monuments
ASIA
BERING SEA
ALEUTIAN ISLANDS
ARCTIC OCEAN
GREENLAND ICE SHEET
Queen Elizabeth Islands
Victoria Island
Baffin Island
Great Bear Lake
Great Slave Lake
L. Athabasca
Wood Buffalo NP
HUDSON BAY
LABRADOR SEA
NORTH PACIFIC OCEAN
GULF OF ALASKA
Bering Land Bridge NM
Noatak NM
Gates of the Arctic NM
Brooks Range
Yukon River
Denali NM/Mt. McKinley NP
Katmai NM
Lake Clark NM
Mt. McKinley
Anchorage
Yukon-Charley NM
Wrangell-St. Elias NM
Mt. Logan
Glacier Bay NM
Mac Kenzie R
ROCKY MOUNTAINS
Fraser R
Vancouver
Puget Sound
Olympic NP
Mt. Rainier
Jasper NP
Banff NP
Yoho NP
Kootenay NP
Waterton Lakes NP
Glacier NP
Prince Albert NP
Riding Mt NP
L. Winnepeg
Columbia R
Flathead L
Ft Peck Res
Yellowstone NP
Yellowstone R
Missouri River
Cascade Range
Cape Mendocino
Mt. Shasta
Sierra Nevada
GREAT BASIN
San Francisco Bay
San Francisco
Yosemite NP
Sequoia/Kings Canyon NP
Mt. Whitney
Death Valley NM
Great Salt Lake
Rocky Mtn NP
Platte R
Colorado River
Canyonlands NP
Grand Canyon NP
Arkansas River
Red River
Rio Grande
Big Bend NP
L Superior
L. Michigan
L Huron
L Ontario
L Erie
Chicago
Mississippi River
Ohio R
Great Smoky Mtns NP
Tennessee River
APPALACHIAN MTNS
St Lawrence River
Gulf of St Lawrence
Montreal
Cape Cod
New York
Chesapeake Bay
Cape Hatteras
NORTH ATLANTIC OCEAN
L Okeechobee
Everglades NP
GULF OF MEXICO
CENTRAL AMERICA
CARIBBEAN SEA
Ice
Tundra
Mountainous
Northern Coniferous Forest
Mixed Coniferous & Deciduous Forest
Plains & Grasslands
Deserts & Chaparral

INTRODUCTION
Isaac Asimov

For those of us who are enamored of life in all its forms; who see our planet as a vast and awesome network of ecological balance; who are fascinated by the grace and beauty of all the products of long evolution; this is the best of times—and the worst of times.

It is the best of times because all the world is now open to us, so that we can, and do, study the entire panorama of living things in its majesty. Furthermore, we have the techniques required to freeze instants, to catch on film those exquisite moments that in real life would pass us in a flash.

These techniques enable us—each of us—to see what otherwise only the expert—after what may be a long and most uncomfortable, even dangerous, wait—could see. We can see it at our leisure and return to it over and over, for there is no danger of something, as intricate and marvelous as living organisms in their millions of varieties, ever wearing out its welcome. This book on North American wildlife is evidence of that.

North America is, of course, *our* continent. It is a relatively new continent to humanity, which has occupied it for 25,000 years, as compared with anywhere from 500,000 to several million years for the continents of the Old World.

Fortunately for ourselves, its characteristic life-forms are distinctly different—and magnificent.

Nearly two centuries ago, Baron Cuvier, the great French naturalist, had a rather poor opinion of North American wildlife. Judging from what he had seen, he decided that the animals of North America were small and degenerate copies of those of the Old World. When President Thomas Jefferson heard of this, he had a moose stuffed and sent to Cuvier. Cuvier took one look at the monster—the largest member of the deer tribe that exists—and admitted his error.

Here is a book that is particularly designed to show all similar disparagers the error of their ways. You will see the vigor, not only of the large animals such as the moose, Kodiak bear, musk ox, bison, bighorn, but of the small animals such as the coyote, jack-rabbit, and raccoon, each of which is a triumphant example of the one quality for which evolution awards its prize—the ability to survive.

And yet it is also the worst of times.

Humanity, in its restless expansion, particularly over the last two centuries, has been crowding remorselessly against the natural habitats of wildlife. Species are becoming extinct at a terrifying, and still accelerating, rate. We actually face the prospect of seeing an end to all the larger and more imposing forms of wildlife within a matter of decades.

If this be so, we will lose something that cannot be replaced. It is not only that much that is beautiful will be forever gone, and that all of us will be poorer for that. Much more appalling is the fact that we are not sure just how the loss of so much of the fabric of life will affect what is left. There is an intricate interdependence of life that involves *us,* too, and with the web slashed and demolished, we cannot be certain how far our own ability to live will be impaired, or how far the very viability of the planet will be compromised.

This book you hold, then, is not only the evidence of what can be presented to this generation, as it could never be presented to earlier ones—but as it may never be presented to later ones, either.

It may also help inspire you with the feeling that wildlife must *not* be allowed to perish from the Earth. The more you admire the beauty of the photographs and revel in the words of the text, the more you must surely feel that all this should be preserved for your children and grandchildren as well.

Below: A pair of bull moose, largest member of the deer family, swim a river in Alaska. Baron Cuvier's low opinion of North American wildlife improved dramatically upon his receiving a stuffed moose from President Thomas Jefferson.

THE ARCTIC

Polar Bear

The polar bear, king of the North, may weigh 1,000 pounds and measure eight feet from nose to tail. The large individual is five feet high at the shoulders, and standing erect on its broad hind feet, may tower 12 feet above the ground—twice the height of a tall man.

Not only are these magnificent animals unbelievably powerful, they are also unpredictable, a combination that makes them dangerous, especially when they are caught by surprise, or when a female with cubs is approached. Furthermore, the polar bear may show little fear of people where protected from shooting. In Churchill, Manitoba, which lies on a polar bear migration route, the white bears become accustomed to roaming through the center of town, feeding at the dumps, walking through the streets poking their snouts into open doors, and causing human parents to keep their eyes on their children.

Through most of their wide range, however, the polar bears belong to the wilderness. They live in the Arctic regions of five countries, Canada, the United States, the USSR, Denmark (Greenland), and Norway. Problems for the polar bear intensified when men with guns began invading the Arctic. Today the five nations with polar bears have an agreement that helps protect the bears. Joint commissions study the bears and cooperate in setting regulations that affect them. Even with this protection, the polar bear is in trouble; its numbers probably total fewer than 20,000 animals scattered over the vast northern seas.

These sea-going bears are seal hunters and their major prey is the ringed seal which weighs, when grown, 100 pounds or more. The polar bear has two basic seal hunting techniques. One is to lie in ambush beside the seal's breathing hole. As the seal surfaces to breathe, which it must do frequently, a giant paw flashes out with amazing swiftness and crushes the seal's skull. Then, its

Opposite: The polar bear close up.

Below: A female polar bear and her cub.

body is quickly snatched from the icy water. Any edible parts of its meal that the polar bear leaves behind, the Arctic foxes and ravens soon clean up.

The other method for hunting is to slip up on sleeping seals. When a seal rests on the surface of the ice, it must be constantly alert for the hunting bear, sleeping only a few minutes at a time, then lifting its head to survey the scene. While the seal is looking, the stalking bear freezes in place and waits for the seal's head to drop again. Then the bear makes another cautious advance, taking advantage of ice ridges to help hide its movements. The perfectly camouflaged bear often, but not always, gets close enough to rush the seal before it can escape back to the water.

Polar bears spend large parts of their lives drifting on ice floes over the northern waters. In this manner they may drift several hundred miles a year, traveling with the currents even through the long, dark winter.

Meanwhile, the female about to bear young is not drifting with the ice, but instead is snugly hidden in a den. The expectant female has moved inland and chosen a steep bank where the snow will drift and cover her well. She hollows out a room, but keeps a breathing hole open and her snow shelter becomes a cozy sanctuary in the bitter North Country.

In the dead of winter she gives birth to her young, usually twins, each of them weighing about a pound and a half. The tiny cubs are blind and helpless, but by the end of winter they are big enough to leave the den with their mother and wander off over the surrounding countryside.

No one should ever make the mistake of thinking he or she can out-run a polar bear. The bear can lumber along at speeds of 35 miles an hour. It is also at home in the water, where it can swim at six miles an hour and may travel for a hundred miles or more, sometimes with nothing but its black nose sticking above the surface. The mother may let her cubs hitch a ride on her back as she swims.

The polar bear possesses a sense of smell so keen that Eskimos insist the bear smells odors from miles away.

In recent times, polar bears have been the subject of extensive field studies by biologists who want to know more about the needs of the bears and how they can best be protected from the modern hazards they face. These studies, often using small transmitters which emit signals that can be followed by airborne biologists, have brought us new information on how the bears of the Far North live and where their travels take them.

For two and a half years they stay with their mother, learning to capture their food. The female gives birth to new young only every second year, leaving her sufficient time to care for her cubs until they can survive alone.

The giant bear is well outfitted for life in the Arctic. It wears a thick coat of long, white hair and even the soles of its feet are covered with hair. Beneath the skin lies a layer of fat, sometimes four inches thick, that serves as both insulation and a source of energy.

Below: A male polar bear on Alaska's ice pack stands guard over his fresh kill.

Above, top and bottom: In these rare photos an Alaskan polar bear feeds on the carcass of his prey.

Wolf

The howl of the wolf is unforgettable. Low and mournful, it rolls across the tundra or through the northern forest. The wolves which once ranged over nearly all of the North American continent are now restricted to the remote regions of the Arctic and a few other remnants of their original range to the south. Wherever these powerful wild canines have lived close to people there have been rigorous campaigns to destroy them. As a result, wolves vanished quickly as white settlers advanced across North America.

There remain today few places where the traveler may reasonably expect to catch a glimpse of a truly wild, free-roaming wolf pack. Perhaps the best possibility is Denali National Park in Alaska. Wolves also live in a more or less balanced relationship with the moose herd in Isle Royale National Park, on an island in Lake Superior. Visitors to this park, however, seldom see the elusive wolf.

The wolf is still common in parts of Alaska, and lives there in country open enough so that it is frequently seen, especially by pilots, when there is snow covering the ground. Aircraft-borne hunters have made inroads on the Alaskan wolf population, legally and illegally, for sport, and because of the value of wolf fur. Modern laws and game management principles offer an element of protection for this wilderness canine.

A wolf resembles, both in size and in general appearance, a very large German shepherd. The fur is thick, the color may vary widely from dark to light, and a single wolf pack may have individuals that are dark colored, grayish, white or reddish brown. The largest wolves stand three feet high at the shoulder and weigh 100 pounds or more. Females are usually ten to fifteen pounds lighter than their mates. The wolves of the Arctic tend to be lighter in color and somewhat larger than their cousins to the south.

Wolves mate for life. The female wolf usually breeds for the first time at the age of 22 months. About two months later, usually in mid-May, she gives birth to a litter averaging five to seven pups, and each year thereafter adds a new litter to the wolf population. By mid-summer both pups and adults leave the den and begin ranging for considerable distances on hunting

Above: A wolf shivers after a swim in an Alaskan river.

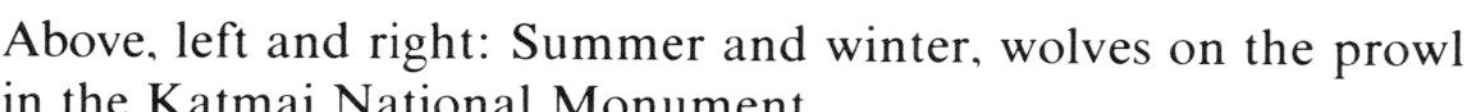

Above, left and right: Summer and winter, wolves on the prowl in the Katmai National Monument.

trips. During the first winter the young wolves will grow to be as large as their parents and become capable of killing larger animals.

Wolves are social animals and normally live in packs which may be composed of animals that are related. The size of a wolf pack will vary, and on occasion, groups of 35 or 40 travel together. But generally the wolf pack is smaller, often containing only six or eight individuals. By hunting in packs, wolves are better able to pursue and kill the large animals on which they subsist.

In the Arctic, moose and caribou are taken by wolves, and this has brought the wolf into conflict with human hunters who want the large game animals for themselves. Biologists believe that the wolf is important to the continued health of the caribou herd, however. The caribou lives on slow-growing lichens and travels constantly in search of food. The wolf helps hold caribou herds within the carrying capacity of their food supply. In addition, the wolf is believed to help keep the prey species healthy and vigorous by removing the weak and disabled individuals. Wolves often add other foods to their diet. They will eat berries, water-fowl, small mammals and fish. Whatever its food, the wolf usually takes only what it needs. It lives on an energy budget and energy used must be replaced by foods taken.

Musk Ox

The musk ox has the longest hair of any wild animal in North America—and needs it. This animal survives in the continent's harshest climate. To see a wild, free-roaming, musk ox you must travel north beyond the Arctic Circle where the winter winds sweeping off the Arctic seas may send temperatures plummeting to 50 or 60 degrees below zero.

These frigid winds drive most creatures to earth to hibernate, or send them migrating south to spend the winter in warmer climates. But the musk ox does neither. The animal is covered with one of the world's finest blankets, a thick wool undercoat, protected by a layer of outer guard hairs that are sometimes two feet long. The whole coat forms a blanket that hangs down to the creature's ankles and covers every part except hoof, horns, and nose. In summer the thick fur coat gives protection from relentless hordes of mosquitoes.

Male and female musk oxen look much alike. Both have dark brown fur, with lighter colored fur on their legs that looks like dirty white socks. They are hump-shouldered, and both sexes carry massive horns that form plates over the front part of their heads then curve down and forward. Eskimos once used these horns as water dippers.

The feet of the musk ox are equipped with hooves with sharp outer edges allowing the feet to cut into crusty snow and give the animal a good grip. The back of the hoof, however, is padded and this gives added traction, making the musk ox sure-footed on rocky or icy surfaces. The musk ox is noted for its agility.

Long ago there were far more musk oxen than there are today. Old records tell the story. Samuel Hearne, who traveled the

Above: A musk ox.

Above: A pair of musk oxen.

Arctic in the late 1700s, reported that in 1795 he went overland to the Copper Mine River where the animals were abundant. Hearne saw them in herds of 100 or more.

Today they are gone from much of their former range. By the mid-1800s, musk oxen had vanished from Alaska. There remain small herds of them in the Canadian Arctic, perhaps 10,000 in all of Canada. Musk oxen can be captured and transplanted, however, and in 1936, 31 of them were brought from Greenland to Alaska and released on Nunivak Island National Wildlife Refuge where today there are several hundred. More recently, musk oxen from this herd have been transplanted to wildlife refuges on the Alaskan mainland.

The natural enemy of the musk ox is the wolf, but the musk ox does not fall victim easily. Musk oxen live in herds and this gives them added protection. When confronted by wolves or other enemies, including people, they form a circle of defense, pushing together so that their heads all face out while the smaller calves take refuge in the center or beneath the adults. The attackers must deal with massive horns. The wolves are safer if they can cut an individual out of the group or perhaps encounter an old lone male no longer living with the herd.

Men from whaling ships proved to be the greatest enemy the musk ox ever met. Hunting crews sought out the animals for the meat they provided and killing them was relatively easy because instead of running, they formed their defensive circle and stood their ground, making it easy for the hunters to shoot them.

The mature male musk ox weighs 500 to 800 pounds and the females are somewhat smaller. They are heavy bodied animals, standing five feet or higher at the shoulders and measuring seven or eight feet in length.

The musk ox has few close relatives among the world's mammals. Scientists consider it more related to sheep and goats than to the bovines.

The female musk ox generally gives birth in April or May, to a single calf every second year and the 20 pound infant is already covered with warm fur to protect it against the bitter winds. The youngster may nurse for 15 months, through that first hazardous winter when food is difficult to obtain. This does not mean that the calf ignores vegetation. It begins, even when a few days old, to pick at the grasses and shrubs that its mother eats, and by the age of four months much of its food is what it gathers for itself.

The truly wild musk ox is as much a symbol of the Arctic as the wolves that pursue it. It belongs on the open tundra where bitter cold winds whip around its shaggy sides and its food lies waiting below crusts of snow and ice that must be scraped away. This is the setting in which musk oxen evolved, perfectly matched for the harsh conditions in which the first Arctic explorers discovered them.

Above: Photographing musk oxen on Nunivak Island, Alaska.
Below: A herd of musk oxen huddle for warmth.

Wolverine

The wolverine is known as a solitary traveler of the far north. It is a member of the weasel family, the *Mustelidae,* and the largest of the group, with the exception of the sea otter. The wolverine stands 15 inches high at the shoulder and weighs 20 to 35 pounds, sometimes more. It is typically about 40 inches long. The head of the wolverine is compact and its ears are small, which is characteristic of mammals that live in the earth's coldest regions.

The shaggy fur coat worn by the wolverine has a dark brown color. A lighter stripe of fur extends along each side from the shoulder to the rump. The wolverine's broad, low-slung body travels on short legs with feet that seem large for its bulk. The large feet are snowshoe type aids in winter travel when the wolverine must cross snow fields.

Wolverines seem content to live their lives apart from all others of their kind. They travel alone the year around, except during the breeding season. In this period, usually in March, the males and females consort briefly before going back to their solitary travels.

In June or July, the female moves into her selected denning place, usually in a thicket or pile of rocks, and there gives birth to two or three young. Throughout that first summer the young wolverines stay with their mother, learning to find and capture food.

The food of the wolverine is varied, for this creature is an opportunist, eating almost anything that lives or has lived. Even the porcupine, covered with its protective spines, is sometimes killed and consumed by wolverines, and the wolverines, in turn, are sometimes killed by the spines.

Above: A wolverine on the attack.

In addition to learning to hunt, the young wolverines become fighters, seemingly unafraid of other animals, large or small. The female wolverine will even attack bears that threaten her young. There is, however, no record of wolverines attacking humans.

This animal, with amazing strength for its size, is capable of moving carcasses that outweigh it many times. There is a record of one wolverine known to have dragged a dead Dall sheep for a mile and a half across the rough tundra of Denali National Park in Alaska, although the sheep weighed five times as much as the wolverine. A wolverine has been known to reduce the contents of a trapper's cabin to rubble.

The amazing strength of a wolverine has aided it in killing animals several times its own size. It has been known to attack and kill deer and even small moose, although these kills probably occurred when the prey animals were bogged down in deep snow and unable to flee or fight back.

By autumn the young wolverines must be able to care for themselves because the female casts them out and resumes her lonely life of solitary wandering. These travels may take her over a wide area. Eskimos report that wolverines have regular routes which they follow in their hunting, and that only once in eight or

ten days do they pass the same point on their trail. If, in these travels, the wolverine discovers a trapper's trap line it may follow the trail, methodically robbing each trap of its catch in turn, until the trapper either outwits the wolverine or, more probably, moves his trap line to a new location.

The wolverine, even in the severest climates, does not hibernate, but continues to roam, searching for food.

The wolverine is a special prize for the northern trapper. Eskimos cherish the fur; it is especially valued for use around parka hoods because this fur does not collect frost.

Above: An arctic fox at rest in an Alaskan snowbank casts a wary eye toward the photographer.

In North America the range of wolverines extends from the Polar Islands south into the Canadian provinces. In the west these animals are also found in California, but they are rare. There are no longer wolverines east of the Rocky Mountains. Even in the best of northern wolverine country this powerful, bear-like animal, with its bad temper and insatiable hunger, populates its range thinly.

Arctic Fox

In the bitterly cold Arctic lives a little fox that survives on what it can capture and scavenge. These foxes of the Eskimo Country have a dull brown coat in summer which changes in August and September to the beautiful pure white fur they will wear into winter as a perfect match for the snowy world in which they live.

In another color phase the Arctic fox has a dingy brown summer coat which, just before winter, changes to a sleek coat of bluish gray. Naturalists have noticed that these blue foxes live largely around the coastal cliffs and feed on colonies of nesting birds while the white foxes depend heavily on lemmings for their food.

The white winter coat of the Arctic fox has high value on the world markets and as the new season arrives the trappers prepare for the fur harvest. The fur of the blue foxes is also valuable and some Alaskan islands have been stocked with blue foxes that devastated the native birds.

In summer, living is easy for the fox. Snow is gone from the tundra, or most of it, and prey animals, especially lemmings, can be readily captured. Ground-nesting birds and their eggs are also taken.

When the harsh winter comes, deep cold settles over the North Country. Layers of ice and snow lock up the frigid land and the fox can neither hibernate nor migrate but must instead stay and make the most of the Arctic winter. It conserves energy by resting through some of the stormy weather. But it must find food, and for this it has two sources. First comes the food cached during times of plenty. Sea birds have been captured and stored for winter and so have their eggs. Many foxes are found living around cliffside colonies where birds nest by the thousands. Other foods are stored as well. The fox's cache is protected from larger predators by storage in rocky crevices.

Stored foods, however, seldom see the Arctic fox through the winter. It must still get out and hunt for food. Foxes trail polar bears, feeding on scraps where the bears kill seals. They even slip along cautiously behind the powerful wolves, searching for leftovers. Along the coast they feed on carrion—dead seals and stranded whales.

In years of lemming abundance the foxes increase their production, and give birth to larger litters. These little wild dogs of the North Country have a litter of young in May and sometimes a second family in August. Each new litter brings four to six infant Arctic foxes into the world to wander over the barren grounds, snowy shores and pack ice, alert for any food that will support them through another difficult winter.

Above: A small portion of a giant herd of Pacific walruses bask in the warmth of the Alaskan sun.

Walrus

The walrus is a huge marine mammal that may weigh 100 pounds or more when newborn and 750 pounds by the time it is two years old. When the female reaches her full size, she will tip the scales to a ton while her mate may weigh two tons.

These gigantic animals of the shallow northern waters are related to seals and sea lions. The walrus is known for its ivory tusks, which are canine teeth protruding from its jaws. Both males and females have tusks. Although the tusks are used in fighting, and to help the walrus pull its bulk up on ice floes, some scientists believe their main use is to help the walrus dig on the shallow ocean floor for food.

The walrus has a circumpolar range and scientists recognize two sub-species, the Pacific and the Atlantic. The Pacific walrus is larger and its tusks longer; these are the most obvious differences between it and its Atlantic cousin.

The main food of the walrus is a variety of invertebrate animals that live on the bottom of shallow Arctic waters. Clams are

the mainstay and several different species are eaten by the walrus. The feeding walrus eats only the protruding part of the clam, and scientists believe that this fleshy part is removed by suction. In addition to clams, walruses eat snails, crabs, worms and shrimp which they locate by running their broad, flat muzzles over the ocean bottom. They will also eat fish. Eskimo hunters report that the walrus sometimes eats seals.

In the Pacific they make annual migrations moving south for the winter and north again as soon as warming weather breaks up the ice. A walrus in a spring migration may travel as far as 2,000 miles and it is during this migration, in late April or early May, that the Pacific walruses have their new calves. For at least the next year and a half, and perhaps for considerably longer, the young walruses must be cared for by their mothers. Females begin breeding when six or seven years old and thereafter give birth to a single calf every second year. The breeding season comes during February and March but, as with other pinnipeds, the fetus does not begin to develop immediately. After a few months it begins to grow and later the baby walrus is born.

The walrus has long been important to the Eskimo people.

Above: Some walruses play while the broken tusked patriarch dozes.

The favorite time for killing them comes in spring and summer and for some Eskimo villages the walrus hunt is a time of celebration.

For thousands of years, the walrus supplied the needs of Eskimos who hunted them, apparently without being seriously reduced in numbers. Then came the American whalers, especially during the decade 1860 to 1870, and they were a serious new threat to the animals. In more recent years, Eskimo hunters have used motor driven boats and powerful rifles. Biologists report that a large percentage of walruses shot either sink to the bottom or escape to die later of their wounds. Modern wildlife management and harvest regulations have attempted to restrict the walrus kill to a level below the annual rate of increase. There is wide belief among scientists that walruses were once much more abundant than they are today, and that their habitat could still support more of these giant sea-going mammals than now live in the wild.

Caribou

An Arctic traveler looking to the hills on a summer day may see the wild deer of the Far North, its massive antlers etched against the shimmering sky. No matter how many times caribou have been observed before, sighting one of these magnificient mammals is always exciting. But reactions may vary. The Eskimo hunter reaches for his rifle while the photographer considers stalking the animal for a close up picture and others simply stand and watch to see what happens next.

Shortly the big bull caribou, holding his antlers level, trots off, attempting to escape the persistent insects that will not let him rest. If the caribou does not see the watcher, it may trot down

the slope, sometimes passing so close that the castanet-like clicking of the animal's footbones is plainly audible.

On other occasions the caribou arrive, both in small groups and in large herds numbering in the thousands, but always they are on the move. Except for that brief period in early summer when the cows assemble on the calving grounds to drop their new crop of young ones, the restless caribou spend much of their lives traveling.

The Arctic wildlife community is noted for the small number of species that comprise its frequently astounding biomass. Early northern travelers on the Yukon River told of steamboats, halted for hours because the stream was choked with migrating caribou swimming across the Yukon. In 1900 Canada might have held as many as two million Barren Ground caribou. A fraction of that number wander the Canadian Arctic today and in Alaska too, caribou numbers have fallen drastically for reasons not fully understood.

The historic Porcupine Herd is shared equally by the United States and Canada. These animals migrate down into the foothills of the Brooks Range in Alaska to have their new calves and spend much of the summer on the Douglas National Wildlife Range before moving back into the hills of Canada for the winter. In recent years the Porcupine Herd, and caribou almost everywhere, have seen their native range invaded by people in search of oil and other valuable resources.

Nature has winterized the caribou, preparing it for life in a land where winter temperatures fall to 50 degrees or more below zero while bitter winds whip skeins of snow across the open tundra. The caribou's fur coat is among the world's most effective insulators. Composed of hollow hairs filled with insulating dead air, the coat locks out winter winds, a snug fur wrap that conserves precious energy needed to survive the cold months. In addition, the caribou's feet are especially adapted to life on the icy northern snowfields where its broad spreading hoofs support it.

The caribou's major food source is the lichens that carpet the tundra for mile after mile. In winter the broad hooves become

Opposite: A caribou bull stands his ground.
Above: The glow of the sunset washes the slopes of the Brooks Range as a caribou herd passes on its annual migration.
Below: A younger caribou makes his way down a slope.

snow shovels helping uncover the lichens. In summer the diet also includes willows and other vegetation.

The wandering caribou may have to work hard to find enough lichens to meet their energy needs. The lichens grow slowly, taking many years to grow only a few inches high. The caribou follow no regular routes between summer and winter areas. Even the Eskimos never know when the deer are coming or where they will appear next and this pattern of grazing allows the lichens time to recover before the grazers reappear, perhaps years later.

For centuries the Eskimos, especially those living inland away from the coast, have relied heavily on the caribou. Not only did they take the meat for food, as they still do, but they also used the hide for clothing. Seven skins were enough to fashion a suit for the hunter. In the coldest weather he wore two suits, an inner suit with the fur against the body and an outer one with the fur facing outside. The skins also covered kayaks and shelters, while the bones were fashioned into tools.

Modern developments brought still greater drains on the caribou herds. Rifles were more efficient than primitive weapons, while ski mobiles outdistanced dog sleds. Modern foods also enabled hunters to stay longer in the field and pursue the caribou at greater distances from the hunters' homes. Fire was an increasingly serious enemy after the coming of white people, for fire destroys the lichens.

Natural enemies of the caribou include the wolves which have lived with the Arctic deer and helped shape their nature for countless centuries. Wolf packs travel with the migrating herds taking an animal from them when they must have food. Often, but not always, the caribou selected are those most easily caught, the young, the old and those weakened by injury or disease. Barren Ground grizzly bears will also take caribou on occasion.

In addition to the Barren Ground caribou there are, to the south, the woodland caribou living across the continent from the Maritime Provinces to British Columbia. These animals, closer to civilization, have fared even less well than their Barren Ground cousins.

Top: A caribou herd on the move
Above: A migrating herd fords a river in northern Canada.
Below: A bull with a magnificent rack of antlers enjoys a summer forage.
Opposite, top: A bull with his antlers in velvet.
Opposite, bottom: A newborn calf tries his spindly legs.

The Rocky Mountains

Grizzly Bear

Ancestors of today's grizzly bears came to North America by plodding over the Bering Sea land bridge from Asia during the Ice Age. The giant bears advanced eastward and southward as far as what is now Nebraska, Kansas, the Dakotas, and Texas. They flourished in California and south into Mexico.

Today the grizzly bear is gone completely from most of that original range, and typically its numbers are pitifully low where it survives. There have been no grizzly bears reported in California since 1922. Only a remnant hangs on in the mountains of Mexico while a few western states can still boast relict populations secluded in their most remote wilderness mountain ranges. On rare occasions, visitors to Yellowstone National Park sight an unforgettable grizzly bear, but the largest number live in the wilderness regions of Alaska and Canada.

Neither grizzly bears nor people have adapted gracefully to each other's presence. Ranchers have historically viewed the grizzly as a livestock-killing enemy. Grizzly bears have killed and injured people who invade bear country. In the few national parks where conditions remain wild and natural enough to maintain populations of these powerful bears, there is an uneasy truce between people and the grizzly.

The adult grizzly is an awesome animal, often weighing 600 pounds, or sometimes more than half a ton. It stands four feet high at the shoulders, has a large head with a dish-shaped face and a hump on the shoulders. The fur varies in color but yellowish brown is a common color among grizzlies.

The grizzly is equipped with long, only slightly curved, claws on its front feet. The hump on the shoulders, the shape of the

Opposite: A pair of grizzlies.
Below: A mother grizzly and her cubs.

Left: A Grizzly fishing in Glacier National Park.
Above: A pair of grizzlies grazing.

face and its size set it apart from its smaller and more common cousin, the black bear.

One secret of the grizzly bear's success as a wild forager and hunter is the wide variety of food it finds acceptable. As the largest of the world's carnivores, the grizzly bear is capable of killing elk, moose, and other large animals. One swat of a big grizzly bear's giant front paw can break the neck of a steer, after which the powerful bear may carry its victim off where it can cache the surplus for later use.

But most of the grizzly bear's food comes in smaller helpings. It spends more time eating berries and roots than it does stalking elk or caribou. It digs roots, excavates small burrowing animals and takes the young and eggs of ground nesting birds. Fish are a favorite food and the swiftness of the big bears enables them to catch the darting fish in shallow waters.

Grizzly bears commonly travel alone. Once every second or third year the females accept the company of the males, and for a few weeks, they travel together, sometimes rolling and tumbling in their play.

Then, with the early winter storms, the female takes refuge in her favorite den and there, in the dead of winter, gives birth to her young ones, usually twins, which weigh about a pound and a half each and are naked, blind, and completely helpless when born. In the spring, the young bears emerge from the den to begin traveling with their mother, playing, growing and learning. Young grizzly bears, unlike mature ones, are capable of climbing trees if threatened.

The cubs stay with the female until they are in their second year. The grizzly matures to its full size in eight to ten years and may live well into its twenties.

Those who invade the forests and tundra where grizzly bears live should for their safety, remember that they share the land with the big bears. Although grizzlies are thinly spread through their range, there is always the possibility of rounding a curve in the trail and surprising a bear as it feeds. Surprising them is the biggest danger with grizzly bears. If they are well warned in advance of the presence of people the bears generally slip away quietly and hikers often carry noisemakers to announce their presence in bear country. But there can be no guarantee; the grizzly is unpredictable.

These giant bears remain wilderness creatures—perhaps the most exciting wild animals in all of North America.

Mountain Lion

Before the arrival of European settlers in North America, the mountain lion was more widely distributed than any other wild mammal on the continent. These native American lions were at home from the Atlantic to the Pacific and from southern Canada southward all the way through Central and South America to Patagonia. Within this range, mountain lions held territories from far up the mountain slopes down to sea level, mostly in the forests, but also in deserts and swamp lowlands.

The mountain lion has since been eliminated from large blocks of this original range. In the United States, they are limited mostly to western states, with minuscule populations still surviving in the Northeast and in the south. The mountain lion is believed to be increasing in some western states.

Among the native cats, the mountain lion is second in size in the Western Hemisphere only to the jaguar. The adult lion, which is also known as cougar, panther or deer tiger, measures about seven feet long from the dark tip of its tail to its nose. The record for size is held by an Arizona mountain lion that weighed 276 pounds. The average male would be closer to 150 pounds, while his mate would weigh about two-thirds as much.

The mountain lion is covered with short smooth hair that is tawny yellow, golden brown or slate gray with whitish underparts. The fur is not spotted in mature animals, but the playful kittens carry large patches of dark hair and also have rings around their tails. The ears are small and erect. This American lion, traveling on large padded feet, moves quietly and stalks its prey in near silence.

They do not form permanent pair bonds but spend their lives roaming as individuals. The adult female breeds every two or three years.

Above: A mountain lion shows her fangs.
Below: A pair of mountain lions crouch in their lair.

Ninety-six days after the mating, the female mountain lion gives birth to her litter of kittens, an average of three, and they may be born in any season. Spring-born litters, however, are the most common. This brings the young cats into the world when prey animals are having their young, thereby increasing the possibility of survival for these predators.

The mother cougar hides her kittens among boulders or in a pile of downfallen timber in a remote canyon. Their eyes are closed in the early days of their lives, but begin to open when they are nine or ten days old. When the young ones are two or three months old, they will begin to travel with their mother on her hunting trips. They are learning to support themselves by hunting.

The young stay with the mother for two years and when she casts them out, they must locate and occupy their own hunting territories. The search, often long and difficult, may end up a hundred miles or more from where it began. Once mountain lions have established territories, they mark the boundaries with scratch piles of litter which they scent with urine. The territory of a single lion in the Rocky Mountains may cover as much as 75 square miles.

The mountain lion hunts at night, often by traveling the ridges. During a single night's hunting it may travel 25 miles. Hunting is difficult work. The cat frequently fails in its efforts to make a kill.

The most important element in the mountain lion's diet, under natural conditions, is deer meat. When deer prosper, the lions may do well also. Studies show that some western mountain lions need a yearly supply of 14 to 20 deer, plus perhaps half a dozen elk. With its venison, the mountain lion will also consume smaller prey including raccoons, rabbits, birds, frogs and fish. It even eats porcupines after flipping them onto their backs so it can kill them but escape the danger of the quills. The mountain lion also takes domestic stock on occasion, and this has made the shepherd and cattleman historic enemies of the cougar.

Studies in Idaho, in the Salmon River wilderness country, proved that eliminating the mountain lions did not result in larger deer and elk herds. Instead, the deer herds are limited, not so much by predation as by shortages of winter food.

Mountain lions are earning greater respect today than ever before through the American West. Historically, cattlemen have viewed cougars as vermin and shot them on sight. They are run with hounds until they tree and can be shot.

Today, however, the mountain lion has graduated, in many states, from the status of vermin to the level of a respected game animal, giving it added protection by conservation officers.

Above: At rest in a snow-covered pine.
Below, right: A mountain lion guarding its kill.
Below, left: A Utah mountain lion on the hunt.

Meanwhile, because of the growing interest in mountain lions and other wildlife, especially species in danger, there has been recent research into the life secrets of these magnificent predators. Some biologists even hope to reintroduce mountain lions into wilderness areas from which they have vanished.

Those who are fortunate may catch a fleeting glimpse of the elusive free-roaming mountain lion or discover the print of its foot in the soft earth of the forest. But whether we see the giant cat or not, there is satisfaction in knowing that North America's native lion still survives in the wildest canyons.

Bobcat

The bobcat stays out of sight, hiding in the thickets and lurking in the shadows. As a result, most people have never seen a wild bobcat and perhaps never will.

If, however, the bobcat were to pose in plain view, you would see an animal that measures about three feet long and weighs 15 to 25 pounds. The male is generally 25 percent larger than the female. This cat has a short stubby tail and its erect ears are decorated with tufts of fur. Biologists believe these bits of fur extending from the tips of the cat's ears give it better hearing than it would otherwise possess.

The animal may look larger than it is because of its fluffy coat. The coat is yellowish brown to reddish brown and somewhat spotted. Its winter coat is more of a grayish color.

Bobcats range over a large part of North America, north into Canada where, beyond the bobcat's range, the somewhat larger Canada lynx takes over. Within its range the bobcat occupies a wide variety of habitats from coastal swamps to mountain slopes. Some are desert dwellers.

Bobcats are nocturnal, and as night comes on they emerge from their daytime resting places and begin to hunt. By morning they are back in their secret resting places. They are opportunists and their food may be any of a number of animals including birds, squirrels, prairie dogs, porcupines, rattlesnakes, rats, mice, insects and, on occasion, even fruit. If given a choice, however, the bobcat specializes in catching rabbits which promise it a sizable meal with minimum risk and moderate expenditure in energy.

The hunting bobcat pursues its prey much as the household cat might stalk a bird. It may move silently to the top of a ridge and gently lift itself up until it can see what lies on the other side. If there should be a rabbit grazing in the moonlight, the cat drops silently into its crouching position, then begins stalking. A step at a time, it creeps closer and closer to its prey, keeping its eyes on the rabbit constantly, ready to adjust its tactics if the

Above: A Utah bobcat snarls.
Left: A bobcat in repose.

need arises. If the rabbit looks up, the cat freezes in place until the rabbit, reassured, goes back to munching grass.

The bobcat inches forward, seeming to be in no hurry. At last the cat is crouched in the shadows, unmoving and waiting for exactly the right moment. Then the rabbit lowers its head, and in this instant the cat bounds forward at top speed, closing the distance within a leap or two.

If the rabbit senses the danger quickly enough, it may dart to one side or the other, dash into the thick underbrush, or escape into a hole, leaving the cat frustrated. The cat does not pursue the prey for long but instead gives up the case and hunts another animal. But if the cat has been quick enough, the rabbit rolls beneath it and is quickly dead. Hunting is hard work and energy consuming. There is always the hazard of an injury from the prey animal, and an injured predator may no longer be capable of hunting. Starvation is its reward.

Bobcats are loners. Males and females stay within their own territories. There they hunt and as they make their rounds, mark the limits of their areas with urine and feces. They seem to respect these scent posts rather than engage each other in deadly combat.

Females give birth to one litter of kittens a year, often among a pile of tumbled boulders at the base of a cliff, in a hollow log or beneath the roots and tangled vegetation of a tree that has blown down. There will usually be two or three kittens in the new litter, fur covered, but blind for the first nine days of their lives, and completely helpless. The female alone cares for her kittens. The father is not part of the family.

By early summer, when they are still only partly grown, the kittens begin accompanying their mother on her hunting trips through the night. They have much to learn. By autumn their training ends and they are off to make their own way. This is a critical time and many of the young bobcats will not be efficient enough as hunters to survive through their first winter, especially if the winter is a severe one. During times of heavy storms the bobcat holes up to wait and for several days and nights it may go without food.

Above: A young bobcat.
Below: Montana bobcats inhabit the slopes of the Rockies.
Opposite: A Tennessee bobcat on the prowl for rabbits.

On a winter night male and female meet and the woods are filled with caterwauling, snarling, hissing, squealing and growling much like that of domestic cats but louder. In an hour or so, the two cats separate. The life cycle has begun again, and from 63 to 70 days later the female gives birth to her new litter of kittens, a process she will repeat annually for perhaps 12 or 15 years.

In recent times, the commercial value of spotted cat furs has increased manyfold, and bobcats have suffered extreme pressure from trapping, both legal and illegal. More than ever, the wild hunter has become the hunted.

Moose

The moose is a creature of the northern forests with a circumpolar distribution. It is the largest of the deer family, largest of the earth's antlered creatures, and an impressive animal wherever encountered. The bull may weigh nearly 1300 pounds, stand seven feet high at the shoulders and carry on his head a set of antlers spreading across six feet or more.

He stands on stilt-like legs, has a large hump on his shoulders, a long knobby face, large ears and beneath the head hangs a foot-long dewlap, or bell, that seems to be without purpose. The moose also has a large, overlapping upper lip. The cow is similarly shaped except that she is smaller, has no antlers and her bell is smaller.

Although the moose looks clumsy, it is graceful of movement and capable of slipping into the thickest brush with scarcely a sound. Hikers sometimes pause on the trail when a patch of dark fur moves in the bushes and, as they watch, a giant animal emerges quietly from the brush to stare with its myopic eyes at the intruders.

A moose can provide a major addition to a family's winter food stores. For this reason, the moose was important to ancient people and later to early explorers and settlers. The moose remains an important game animal today.

Above, and opposite lower left: A young moose travels with his mother in Mt. McKinley National Park, Alaska.
Opposite, top and lower right: Moose often forage in swamps, such as this bull, antlers in velvet, in a swamp adjacent to McDonald Creek in Glacier National Park, Montana.

Above: A moose calf nursing. Yukon Flats, Alaska.
Below: A bull moose in a mountain lake in Utah.
Opposite, top: A bull and cow at rest, Grand Teton National Park.
Opposite, bottom: The bull on the move.

In addition, the moose faces danger on highways or railroad tracks. They are frequently killed in winter along railroads in Alaska, and on the Kenai Peninsula the highway deaths of moose have run as high as 250 animals a year.

In the rutting season, bull moose have been known to charge locomotives. Some people believe the train whistle comes through to the attacking moose as the challenge of another bull. Whether such collisions can be credited to poor vision (which the moose has), lack of perfect pitch, or the flowing juices of the mating season, the attacking moose seldom wins an encounter with one of man's vehicles. There is, however, one story of a moose in Alaska that was hit by a train with such force that the moose flew through the air, landed on a switch handle that sent the engine down the wrong spur track where it collided with another train. There were no injuries (except to the moose), but crews needed a week to clean up the derailed equipment.

Two bull moose encountering each other at the peak of the mating season may fight until they suffer injuries. Bushes are knocked down, antlers rattle against each other and grass is uprooted as the two giants maneuver around and around each other, pushing and shoving. If their antlers should lock, the moose may be unable to free themselves, and remain locked together until they starve or are killed by predators. When the breeding season ends in late November, the bulls no longer fight and may even travel together, sometimes with a few cows and calves.

Summer brings choice foods for the moose, especially the aquatic plants in shallow northern lakes. In this season moose are frequently seen standing belly deep in the dark water. The animal dips its long face into the water and comes up showering silvery spray around it while holding in its mouth strands of duck-potato and other plants. It also browses on the leaves and twigs of bushes and trees, especially aspen, willow, maple and birch.

In winter, the food supply is less abundant as snow blankets the north woods. Ice covers the ponds. The moose relies on buds and twigs. Willow and fir may become important foods, depending on what is available. In this season the moose also eats bark that it strips from the aspen trees, sustaining life until spring brings new growth to the woodlands.

For the moose, the life cycle begins in May or June when the cow gives birth to her single calf, or sometimes to twins. The newborn calf weighs 25 to 35 pounds. Within a few days it is nibbling at foods and testing them. By the time the moose is a year old it is mature and can become part of the breeding population. From this time on, the female may give birth annually for up to 18 years.

Wolves have been a major predator on moose in the past and wolves still take moose wherever the two live wild together.

Moose calves fall victim to bears. Grizzly bears probably take even the adult moose on occasion. In addition, moose suffer from various diseases and parasites that may weaken or even kill them. Careful controls must be exercised over hunting to keep the kill from reducing populations below a healthy herd level.

Elk

Deep in the mountain forest or high on an alpine meadow, the stately elk is king of the wilderness. Within the deer family only the lumbering moose outweighs the 800 to 1,000 pound bull elk.

Once the wild elk ranged over much of the northern two-thirds of the United States, all the way from the Pacific coast to

Above: Heavy snowfall in the Rocky Mountains hampers the elks' movements, making them easy prey for predators.
Opposite, top: A magnificent bull with six-point antlers.
Opposite, bottom left: A five-point bull with the beginnings of a sixth point.
Opposite, bottom right: Two bulls, antlers locked in a mating duel.

Below: A big bull in California's central valley.

Left: The bull elk's massive rack of antlers provides him with an awesome offensive as well as defensive weapon. However, when two bulls clash they run the risk of their antlers locking and certain death from preditors if they can't pull free.

the Appalachian mountains. But by the beginning of this century they were gone from much of the land. The elk have since moved back into some of their historic range, however, and the easiest places to see them are in parks and refuges. Yellowstone National Park offers excellent elk watching. So does Wind Cave National Park in South Dakota. But the best of all places is in the National Elk Refuge at Jackson, Wyoming. Here the elk come down from the mountains of Yellowstone National Park and the nearby national forests by the thousands each autumn to winter in the valley, where refuge personnel haul hay to them on horse-drawn sleds. Few wildlife encounters in all of North America are more impressive.

For real elk watchers, however, the favorite season comes in September when the elk are mating. During these golden days, bull elk send their high pitched calls rolling across the mountain slopes and the bugling of the bull elk heard across the Alpine meadows is eerie, unforgettable wilderness music. As the warm autumn sun filters through the yellowing aspens, elk on the mountainsides gather in herds and begin moving gradually toward the low land where winter food will be more easily obtained.

During the winter those magnificent spreading antlers begin dropping from the heads of the bulls. Every year the antlers fall, to be replaced by new ones the following summer. The new crop of calves appears in May and June when there is abundant tender green growth. The birth usually occurs in dense cover where the calves are hidden from predators and protected from the elements.

When the calf is a few days old, the mother takes it with her and returns to her herd of cows and young. Sometimes a single cow may watch over a number of calves, serving as a baby sitter while other cows feed. For four to six weeks the spotted calves grow on their milk diet, gaining strength and agility. In these early weeks they live in constant danger from coyotes, bears, and bobcats. But as they gain size they become increasingly secure.

Opposite, top: Like deer fawns, elk calves, such as these in Yellowstone National Park, are born with distinctive white spots.

Opposite, bottom: In Yellowstone, a mother elk nurses her young calf.

Below: Part of a herd of elk, antlers in velvet, as the early morning fog burns off on the northern California coastal hills of Redwood National Park.

Bighorn

The wild sheep live far up in the mountains where strong winds gust over the high country. These rugged animals with their spectacular curved horns are at home in alpine meadows and on rocky slopes, out of reach of most predators.

There are several kinds of bighorn sheep in North America. The northernmost of the wild sheep are the thinhorn group including the all-white Dall's sheep of the Arctic and sub-Arctic and the closely related Stone's sheep, which wears darker colors and is native to the northern part of British Columbia and southern Yukon Territory. The bighorn group lives to the south and there are three kinds commonly recognized, the Rocky Mountain bighorn, the California bighorn and the increasingly rare desert bighorn. All the North American bighorn sheep are

Opposite: A herd of bighorns grazing on a hillside in Banff National Park, Canada.
Below: A bighorn ram in Montana.
Following page, left: A Dall ram.
Following page, right: A young bighorn in Banff National Park, Canada.

Below: This male bighorn has broken or rubbed off the tip of his curled horn to improve his peripheral vision.

believed to have descended from the wild sheep of northern Asia and it is believed that these sheep arrived on this continent during the Pleistocene Epoch—over the land bridge across the Bering Strait.

The Rocky Mountain bighorn have shorter ears and are larger in size than other bighorns. Their horns are also heavier than are those of the desert or California bighorn.

Bighorn sheep carry true horns that continue to grow throughout the animal's life. The male bighorns develop magnificent curling horns, often with a three-quarter curl by the age of four or five, and 'full curl' horns by the time the ram is nine or 10 years old. These horns, formed of keratin, grow like fingernails. When food is abundant, as it is during the growing season, the horns grow rapidly. In winter, when the animal may have to draw on its stored fat for energy, the horns grow more slowly, and it is the different growth rates that give the outer shell of the horn its corrugated appearance. Biologists can 'read' these rings to determine the age of a bighorn sheep.

The coat of the bighorn is composed of an outer layer of heavy, coarse hair over an inner layer of wool.

Bighorn sheep mature by the time they are a year and a half old, but the young ewes seldom begin breeding until they are two and a half. Meanwhile the young rams must work their way into the ram hierarchy, and the older and stronger males with heavier horns keep the young rams away from the ewes.

The Rocky Mountain bighorn sheep breeding season comes in November and December and once the mating season ends, the males wander off, leaving the females and young to themselves. Bighorn lambs are born in early summer following a gestation period of 175 to 180 days and usually the female gives birth to a single lamb.

This may occur on a narrow rock ledge far above the valley floor. From her high country nursery the wild sheep can keep her vigil, guarding against predators that might threaten her young one. The golden eagle is a threat. If the giant bird casts its shadow over the rocks, the ewe covers her lamb and stands guard. During these early days she feeds the lamb frequently and within a week or so it has grown strong and sure-footed enough to leave the nursery with its mother when they rejoin their little band of ewes and young.

The bighorn's watch against predators is lifelong. But these animals are well protected by their ability to climb plus the fact that they stay in the open places where they can spot danger from a distance. Although bighorns are killed by coyotes, cougars, lynxes, bobcats, wolves and wolverines, their losses to predators are usually low.

Some bighorn sheep are killed in falls, and some are crushed by avalanches. Others succumb to disease. But where the habitat is productive, domestic and ferral animals are controlled, and hunting is carefully regulated, the wild sheep can maintain their numbers.

Below: A bighorn herd at rest.
Opposite: A bighorn ram in Glacier National Park in Montana.
Following page: A group of young rams engage in a little friendly jousting.

Mountain Goat

Of all the North American mammals, none lives in terrain more hazardous than that occupied by the mountain goat. The sure-footed goat is at home on narrow cliffside ledges and rocky, little, hanging alpine meadows. From its first hours the goat leaps from ledge to ledge, scrambles up slopes and stands on the edges of cliffs where the slightest misstep would send it to certain death below.

Because of its preferred habitat, the mountain goat has been safer from people than most wild mammals have. People seldom go where the mountain goat lives and have found little inducement for moving into its harsh world. Even mountain goat hunters are relatively few, partly because of regulations protecting the animals and partly because only the most rugged trophy hunters choose to pursue this king of the high places.

The mountain goat has no close relatives in North America. The chamois, which lives in Europe, is a relative. The range of the mountain goat extends through the mountains of the northwestern part of the continent from Idaho, western Montana and the Cascades of Washington north into Canada and Alaska. The species has also been transplanted successfully.

These animals are easily spotted from a distance because of their pure white coats. The dense wool undercoat, covered by long, white guardhairs is insulation against the bitter winds that sweep over the wild goat's domain. The mountain goat is a

Opposite: A billy close up.
Below and following page: A mountain goat family crosses a slope on a trail in Glacier National Park.

stocky animal with relatively short, strong legs. A big billy may stand three feet high at the shoulders and weigh perhaps 300 pounds, while the nanny may be 20 or 30 per cent smaller. The dark, curved horns are short; even the largest billy goat may have horns only nine inches long. The goat's tail is little more than a stub.

One secret of the mountain goat's ability to live and travel in its rugged world is the size and shape of its feet. The hind hoof of the adult male measures 12 or sometimes 14 inches long, a length that gives the goat the benefit of snowshoes. The hooves have an outer rim of hard, bonelike material but the inner part is a padded cushion that serves the goat well. This cushioned foot provides a shock absorber as well as good traction.

Besides, the goat has a supreme sense of balance, powerful limbs, and apparently a complete lack of fear of high places. It can pick its way along a narrow rocky ledge that leads nowhere and, when the ledge runs out, turn about by half-climbing the sheer wall with its front feet, then go back in the direction from which it came.

Or it can leap from ledge to ledge, traveling either up or down a slope with equal abandon. The mountain goat is capable of jumping across a chasm 10 or 12 feet wide with ease.

This does not mean that the free-spirited mountain goat is always safe in its demanding environment. Goats do slip and fall to their deaths, and nobody knows how often this occurs. The remains are found at the base of cliffs often enough to tell investigators that falling is one cause of mountain goat mortality.

Goats are also lost in avalanches. Somewhere on the towering slopes the snow mass breaks loose and begins to move. The avalanche gains speed quickly, sweeping along trees, rocks and whatever else is in its path. Goats may scramble to safety. If caught by the avalanche, they may come out uninjured or they may be crushed.

In addition, mountain goats face danger from other members of the wildlife community. Their wild enemies are few because of the remote places they live, but where mountain lions roam their world, the big cats are a threat. Another enemy is the powerful golden eagle. Eagles have been seen to snatch very young goats from the rocky ledges, and these birds are also known to knock yearling goats off the cliffs to their deaths. On occasion, coyotes and bobcats also take young goats. These wild enemies, however, must contend with the mother who seldom lets her young one far from her side.

The mountain goat's year begins with the mating season which lasts through November and halfway through December. Late in May or early in June, the females give birth to the young, usually bearing only one. The infants are soon up and about, ready and willing to travel with their mothers and begin learning how to negotiate the cliffsides. They stay with their mothers until the following year when the next crop of kids is due, and then they are forced off on their own.

Severe winters are hazardous for mountain goats, especially young ones less than a year old. As the first storms descend on the mountains, the goats begin to move. They search out both the lower ridges and the lower south-facing slopes where deep snows are least likely to accumulate and where they can find the food plants they will need to see them through the winter. They will return to the high country for summer and fall. And it is in the high mountains, and in little alpine meadows that this wild-spirited animal is most at home.

Opposite and previous page: Mountain goats are particularly abundant on the cliffs of Montana and Colorado.
Below: A billy goat in Olympic National Park.
Following page, left: A mountain goat kid.
Following page, right: Mountain goats scamper across a hillside at Muir Inlet in Glacier Bay National Monument.

America's Grasslands

Bison

The American buffalo, wild cousin of our domesticated cattle, once roamed the continent in unbelievable numbers. Herds of them moved across the prairies in black waves that flowed for days into the valleys, over the hills and out of sight beyond the horizons. There were perhaps 60 million buffalo or bison living on the abundant wild grasses of North America. Nowhere in the world, not even in Africa, has there been a single, large, wild animal in such abundance.

This was the world of the buffalo, *Bison bison,* when Indian people dominated the continent, and when the earliest white people arrived. With that invasion, however, the vast herds of wild buffalo were destined for dramatic changes.

The buffalo had supplied meat, blankets, sinews, tepee coverings, and bone tools for the Indians for centuries. They were a ready source of meat for the newly arrived settlers and herds east of the Mississippi River (buffalo were found as far east as New York) were gone by 1800. By 1830, the much larger herds of the western grasslands were under siege. Hides and meat moved to market as professional buffalo hunters pursued the

Opposite: The awesome bison.
Below: A bison at sunset on the vast Canadian prairie that the great beasts dominated until well into the 19th century.

western herds. In later years mountains of buffalo bones were gathered and hauled off for use in the making of fertilizer.

The herds melted away. Some hunters claimed they could shoot 250 'buff' a day. In 1848 a single firm recorded purchases of 110,000 robes and 25,000 buffalo tongues which were such a delicacy on the market that the animals were frequently killed for the tongues alone. The building of railroads across the west hastened the disappearance of the buffalo. By 1874 the great southern herd was gone, and in 1900, when the animals were at their all-time low, the buffalo was down to some 300 individuals, 250 of them in Canada. Only in Yellowstone National Park were there any longer buffalo left in the United States and even this remnant almost vanished at the hands of poachers.

Then new laws passed by Congress brought some protection to the Yellowstone buffalo. Small numbers of the giant wild bovines were in private herds and many of these were acquired and moved to refuges. Slowly the shaggy beasts began to move back from the edge of the extinction that had threatened them.

Today there are perhaps 35,000 bison across the country, most of them in small, often privately owned, herds. The biggest herd is on the rolling plains of South Dakota's Custer State Park in the Badlands where thousands of people go each year to see them.

The mature buffalo bull may weigh three-quarters of a ton or more and stand five feet high at the hump on his shoulders. The cows, somewhat smaller, may weigh 1,000 pounds. Both sexes have heavy horns with sharp points. The short tail has a tuft of hair on the end, a fly swatter. The buffalo is a powerfully built animal with massive shoulders and a huge, blocky body. The head, neck and front legs are covered with a robe of longer hair, black or dark brown.

In late summer the breeding season arrives. The gestation period of nine and a half months brings a new spring crop of cinnamon-colored calves. The cow normally has a single calf. The new calf is able to keep up with the herd within a couple of weeks, and within a few months, it is harvesting much of its own food as it grazes along with the adults. The old buffalo may live on into its twenties.

Native foods of the buffalo are the short grasses—buffalograss, bluegrass, bluestem, fescue, and grammagrass. Buffalograss, the major food, once covered the central part of North Amer-

Left: A bison grazes along an icy stream in Yellowstone National Park.
Above: A big bull stands his ground.

ica from Mexico to southern Canada, supporting the buffalo through dry summers and bitter winters. In winter, when the grasslands are covered with snow, the buffalo uncover the nutritious dry grasses by pushing snow aside with their muzzles.

Biologists have learned that buffalo normally feed about five times a day, moving along under the leadership of an older cow while calves stay close by their mothers. Between feedings they lie down to rest and chew their cuds.

Once a day, and sometimes more, the herd visits its watering area. In winter, snow becomes a substitute for the watering hole.

Insects are a summer enemy. Buffalo sometimes roll in water holes until they create a mud bath that plasters their bodies and helps ward off the insect attacks. The animals also rub vigorously and repeatedly on trees and rocks. In certain western localities there are boulders once rubbed by so many buffalo that the surface remains shiny a hundred years later and a deep path around the stone is still evident.

The bison remains the symbol of the western plains, a visible link with the age of covered wagons, mountain men, and Indians. The grasslands, however, have been taken over by white-faced cattle and never again will there be those herds of shaggy beasts that once roamed the continent by the millions.

Top: A herd of bison near a geyser in Yellowstone.
Bottom: A mother nurses her calf.
Opposite: Once near extinction, most bison today live on special ranges or preserves where they are flourishing.

Jack Rabbit

Jack rabbits, which are not rabbits but hares instead, are at home in the natural grasslands and some desertlands of North America. These high-jumping mammals are divided into two groups, the black-tailed and the white-tailed jack rabbits, that have much in common, including ranges that overlap. But the white-tailed jack rabbit is considerably larger and can jump farther and run faster than its black-tailed counterpart. No other native mammal except the pronghorn antelope can outrun the jack rabbit. Hopping along at speeds up to 30 or 35 miles an hour, the jack rabbit easily out-distances the hard-running coyote.

The resourceful coyote, however, frequently manages to capture the jack rabbit. The predator may team up with another coyote and together they run the jack rabbit in relays to slow it down. At other times the coyote cuts across the big circle in which the rabbit runs and intercepts it. The coyote may also stalk a dozing jack rabbit and take it by surprise. Or let the rabbit be slowed by age or sickness and the coyote is there awaiting the opportunity.

Other enemies of jack rabbits include bobcats, wolves, foxes, eagles, great horned owls and hawks, while snakes seek out and consume the infant rabbits in the nests. But people are the most destructive of all jack rabbit enemies.

Against its natural enemies the jack rabbit has several advantages. It has exceptional vision and can spot the slightest movement at considerable distance. Besides there is that set of magnificent big ears, one-third the length of the animal's body, which stick up and turn from side to side collecting sounds from all around. The jack rabbit also has effective camouflage with a fur that matches its background. Besides, it has nerves of steel, sometimes sitting tight in its form, waiting for the danger to pass by. The jack rabbit may remain motionless until almost stepped on, then explodes from underfoot with a force that startles the pursuer and gives the rabbit a momentary advantage. At other times the rabbit bounds off far ahead of the enemy.

As it runs, it frequently leaps high into the air, surveying the landscape and keeping tabs on the progress of enemies.

The jack rabbit's ears are believed by scientists to have another advantage. Other desert dwellers seek the coolness of underground burrows to escape the noonday sun, but the rabbit simply sits in its shallow bowl-shaped resting place, perhaps partly shaded by a bush or cactus plant, waiting for the coolness of night, when it goes for food. The noted authority on desert animals, Knut Schmidt-Nielsen, writes 'It is suggested that the very large ears of the jack rabbit can serve as efficient radiators to the cool sky' Jack rabbits seldom drink water but obtain moisture instead from the vegetation they eat, and the matter of survival under hot desert conditions apparently depends, in part, on their ability to keep cool by losing body heat through the large surface of their ears.

Below and opposite: Black-tailed jack rabbits.

A jack rabbit may have several resting places within its territory. Each is a shallow bowl-like form that the rabbit shapes to fit its body. Young jack rabbits begin their lives in a similar shallow depression in the ground.

The animals have a long mating season covering the first several months of the year in the south and lasting a somewhat shorter time farther north. About six weeks after the mating, the female prepares a home for her young by lining a depression in the earth with soft fur pulled from her underside. Onto this fluffy mattress she delivers her young. The black tailed jack rabbit may have half a dozen young ones, but more likely the average of two or three, while the white-tailed jack rabbit's brood may average four young. They arrive already fur-covered and capable of seeing with eyes that are wide open.

During the day, the new mother keeps watch from a distance. She does not approach the nest and risk giving away its location, but normally waits for darkness before going back to nurse her young. By the time the young ones are a few days old, they are ready to begin nibbling grass, and within a few weeks they are weaned and on their own. The female may raise several families during the summer.

Jack rabbits, which may weigh eight to 12 pounds or more and measure two feet in length, are big consumers and this has brought down upon them the displeasure of ranchers whose livestock need the grasses. But even though jack rabbits have been fought with poisons and guns, they are still seen bounding off across the western grasslands leaping four or five feet into the air and accomplishing 20 foot broad jumps when the need arises.

Above: Jack rabbits have proliferated as the numbers of their natural predators have declined. This has resulted in jack rabbits becoming a serious threat to crops in the West.
Right: A white-tailed jack rabbit pauses on his powerful haunches on the prairies of Saskatchewan.

Prairie Dog

Prairie dogs, which are not dogs but members of the squirrel family, once lived by the millions across the grasslands of central North America. When the first settlers moved west, their creaking covered wagons rolled on for miles through prairie dog towns where the little animals sat up on their haunches as they watched—barking warnings to each other. According to old records, one prairie dog town in Texas extended for 100 miles in one direction and 250 in the other. No one knows the total numbers of prairie dogs in a town of this size. It might have been 400 million.

But the big prairie dog metropolis is no more. Government trappers, coming to the aid of ranchers, killed prairie dogs by the millions to save the grass that cattle need and to eliminate prairie dog holes that sometimes broke the legs of unwary livestock. Small prairie dog towns, however, can still be found in a few places, in parks and wildlife refuges.

One of the easiest places today to see wild, free-ranging prairie dogs is Wind Cave National Park in South Dakota. Here the little rodents occupy towns adjacent to the highway from which tourists watch them.

The prairie dogs belong to a complex ecological community. In Wind Cave National Park the prairie community includes the buffalo, coyote, and others which were historically part of the complex world of the prairie dog. The prairie dogs keep the grasses cropped short, enabling them to see quickly any predator approaching by land. Living in a large group, they can warn each other at the first sight of danger. The watchful prairie dog who detects an approaching coyote, or other predator, stands up and barks its warning, then scampers off to its burrow.

The prairie dog is a vegetarian. It eats roots, leaves and seeds. To this it may add occasional insects, even grasshoppers, which it can capture by leaping into the air. These animals spend much of their winter underground, escaping the cold winds and snows.

Left: A prairie dog pauses near his hole.
Above: A female prairie dog stands upright.

The prairie dog invariably has a well-fed appearance. Its plump body is carried on short legs and it has a flattened head with small ears. The tail is short. The prairie dog, which may weigh two or three pounds, fully grown, has a length of 12 to 15 inches and stands five inches high at the shoulders. Its fur is dull brownish gray to cinnamon in color.

Prairie dogs have a long list of wild neighbors eager to eat them. Many of these live right in the prairie dog towns. Among them are rattlesnakes and burrowing owls. In former times the sausage-shaped black-footed ferret lived with the prairie dogs, but the ferrets are gone now nearly everywhere. Ferrets had only one food—prairie dogs—and as the prairie dogs vanished, the ferret could not survive. There are also the coyotes and on occasion badgers which are capable of digging prairie dogs out of their burrows with remarkable speed. Some predators come by air. Hawks and eagles will take prairie dogs at any opportunity.

The underground tunnels in which prairie dogs live are especially well fitted to their needs. Here in the dark, cool tunnels, the little rodents are protected from most predators as well as summer heat and winter cold. The prairie dog first digs a shaft straight down. But after a few feet of this, it carves out a side room which is its guard room. This provides a place to stop and listen in times of danger. As the tunnel turns in new directions, the prairie dog carves out other rooms. One of these is a sleeping room to which the prairie dog brings grasses for a soft bed. Another is used as a toilet. Prairie dog tunnels are easily found because the soil kicked out by the burrowing animal forms a doughnut shaped mound around the entrance. This gives the prairie dog a bit of added elevation when it stands guard. It also serves as a dike to keep out flood waters when heavy rains spread over the flat grasslands.

The prairie dog is especially busy in spring, for this is the season of mating. A month later the females have their litter of young, usually four to six. The young spend their first few months deep in the burrow, then begin coming outdoors to nibble the young, green grass. They learn, almost at once, to sit up and watch for danger, and, like prairie dogs everywhere, to bark their warnings if trouble looms.

When time comes for her to wean her young, the female simply leaves home. She finds an empty burrow in the prairie dog town or digs a new one. Eventually the group of young breaks up and each goes its own way.

Top: This female prairie dog is gathering straw for her nest.
Bottom: Blacktailed prairie dog.
Opposite: Ground squirrels, such as this Columbian ground squirrel in Montana's Glacier National Park, are among the prairie dog's closest relatives.

Above and opposite: Ground squirrels feeding.

Coyote

Coyotes prosper in the face of adversity. The advance of the human tide has caused some species of wildlife to dwindle and vanish, but the coyote has simply changed its lifestyle, quickly adapting and capitalizing on the new situations. Biologists often say, only half jokingly, that coyotes will inherit the world.

The foods this medium sized member of the canine family consumes depend largely on which foods are available. Coyotes will eat rabbits and game birds, but they will also lunch on grasshoppers, snakes, amphibians, birds and their eggs, and prairie dogs. They relish fresh watermelon and canteloupe from the farmer's patch and will eat grapes and other fruit. They will slip up to the farmstead and dine from the dog's dish. Carrion is acceptable. On occasion a coyote will invade the rancher's fields or the farmer's barnyard and kill chickens, ducks or lambs.

As a consequence, the coyote has been detested by many rural people. Sheep ranchers seldom have a kind word for the coyote and frequently blame the little prairie wolf for more damage than it causes. This has led to widespread campaigns to spread poisons and set traps to kill coyotes. The more enlightened modern trend is toward a selective approach to remove the actual trouble causers while leaving other coyotes because they help hold down populations of rabbits and rodents that consume uncounted tons of forage needed for domestic livestock.

Efforts to poison coyotes, especially by the chemical 1080, have reduced their numbers drastically over large areas of the West. The coyote, however, bounces back quickly when pressures are relaxed. It also spreads steadily into new areas. In recent years, the species has spread eastward until it is now found in every state on the continent. Coyotes have adapted to life in and around cities. Toronto, Philadelphia, Los Angeles and other cities have their resident populations of coyotes.

Because of their vocal abilities, coyotes are sometimes called "song dogs," and the call of the coyote adds a wild note to the evening, whether heard from campground or ranchhouse porch. Out on the mountainside the old dog coyote warms up with a few yelps, then lifts his nose to the moon and fills the valley with sharp yips and yaps, followed by doleful wails. There are answering calls, and soon the night is filled with the music of the song dogs. What the calls mean is known only to the coyotes.

The pairs mate for life, and breeding occurs in the middle of winter. Gestation lasts for 63 days. Then the female gives birth to her litter of pups, usually five to 10 of them, all blind and helpless.

The young coyotes venture from their burrow for the first time when they are about three weeks old and their eyes have been open for 10 or 12 days. For the next eight or 10 weeks, however, the young ones stay close to their den where they can dash for safety if threatened. The female may move her family if she feels threatened.

While they are still young, the pups must begin their hunting lessons. Around the den they fight and play with feathers and bones and these games serve to sharpen their reflexes and improve their timing.

Next they begin following their parents on the hunt. They find out, for example, that two coyotes can sometimes succeed in capturing prey where one would fail. A member of the team ambles across the open prairie in plain view while the fascinated prairie dog sits on its haunches, barking warnings to other prairie dogs. Not until it is too late does it realize that another coyote has slipped up from behind.

In addition to people, the coyote has wild enemies with which it must contend. Among its enemies are wolves, mountain lions, disease and parasites. But the alert coyote, strong enough and fortunate enough to out-distance its enemies, may live until it is 13 years old.

Below and opposite: Coyotes on the Great Plains.

Badger

The badger, the digging champion of North American mammals, belongs to the weasel family. But, unlike the sleek and slender weasels, the badger is broad and rather clumsy in appearance. Instead of relying on its ability to hide in small areas, it depends on superior strength, slashing claws and the digging ability for which it is famous.

The badger is 25 to 30 inches long, stands 9 inches high at the shoulder and may weigh 15 or 20 pounds or more. It is a stocky, broad animal with a flattened head. The ears are short and rounded. The tail and legs are also short and the front feet are equipped with powerful slashing claws which not only enable the badger to dig with remarkable speed but also serve it well as weapons against other predators.

The fur of the badger is neither fine nor fancy, but coarse instead. Its shaggy, silvery gray hair with brown and black marks fits very loosely. Dogs that make the mistake of attacking a badger often find that the animal can twist around in its hide and slash them.

The badger's best known skill is its remarkable ability to dig. It can dig itself into the ground in minutes. This is its method of securing food as well. The badgers live on a wide variety of prey, including ground squirrels, moles, gophers, mice, and insects. Snakes are definitely choice food items for them and western badgers do not hesitate to eat rattlesnakes. In the years when prairie dogs were common across the west in vast prairie dog cities, there were always badgers living close by, taking their toll. The hungry badger simply dug out a prairie dog as it wanted it.

Then, as the prairie dogs dwindled, so did the badgers. The range of the badger extends from Michigan and Ohio westward, and from Saskatchewan and Alberta south to Mexico. Although badgers are rare at the eastern limits of their range, they have been reported with increasing frequency in recent years through western Ohio.

Opposite: The badger may be a bit clumsy in appearance, but he can be a fierce fighter.
Above: With their powerful legs, badgers have a remarkable ability to dig.

The badger does much of its hunting at night. In autumn, when it must build up fat to carry it through the winter, it feeds with increasing vigor. It needs the fat because there are long periods when storms keep the badger in its underground refuge where it must rely either on food it has carried into its burrow or on fat stored on its body. Badgers, however, do not go into true hibernation. Instead, they enter into a deep sleep, curled up in their den and on occasion awaken if they become too hungry. By sleeping away much of the winter, badgers conserve energy and survive on less food than they would otherwise need.

Badgers mate in the autumn and females give birth to a single litter each year in May or June. The average litter contains three or four young, born in an underground chamber in a nest of dry grass. At first, the baby badger's eyes are closed and they will remain closed for a month or more. The female brings them food until they are two-thirds grown and old enough to travel with her on her foraging trips. The old male badger is absent from the family party for he leaves the rearing and training of the young to the female.

By the time autumn arrives, the young badgers are about the size of their parents and fully capable of defending themselves against enemies. Wild enemies of the badger are few. Coyotes may kill them occasionally. Most animals, however, are content to leave this tough, hard-fighting animal free to roam where it chooses when it likes.

The badger is covered with gray, grizzled fur and wears a white stripe down the top of its head. It has light spots under the eyes and black on the forehead and cheeks.

Although the badger is a noted consumer of destructive rodents, few ranchers defend it. A horse stepping into a badger hole can break a leg and throw its rider. As a consequence, badgers have been widely poisoned and shot.

Armadillo

The armadillo, looking like a hairless skunk wearing armor, ranges from the southern United States southward into Chile and Argentina. The nine-banded armadillo, one of 20 species, is found through most of Florida and around the Gulf Coast north into Arkansas and across most of Texas and Central America.

The name, of Spanish origin, comes from the tough coat of armor that protects the armadillo. The layer of armor is composed of bone-like scales. The hard shell covers the top of the body—all but the ears and the underparts. There is common belief that the animal, at the first hint of danger, rolls itself into a tight ball. Some species can, but the nine-banded armadillo is not among them. It can, however, curl up somewhat giving some protection to under parts of its body.

In length, the nine-banded armadillo measures 28 to 30 inches, including the tail. It stands from six to seven inches high, and weighs perhaps 12 to 15 pounds.

The armadillo is a noted excavator that has four toes on the forefeet and five on the hind feet, all bearing strong claws. This tendency to dig brings the animal into disfavor with farmers whose horses and cattle sometimes injure themselves by stepping into armadillo holes. Furthermore, the armadillo, in search of insects, eats garden plants, a tradeoff—the insects that armadillo eat are destructive garden pests.

Insects make up most of the armadillo's diet. By flicking its tongue, the armadillo picks up ants, including the detested fire ants of the South, with great rapidity. It also consumes snails, slugs and earthworms as well as amphibians and reptiles.

The armadillo stays out of sight most of the time and usually does its hunting at night.

Home for the young is a soft nest of leaves and grasses collected and carried home by the female. Bedded on this mattress, the female gives birth to her family of remarkable young. The mating season comes in July or August. Even in copulation the armadillo is unusual among quadrapeds. To breed, she lies on her back. Development of the young is delayed, and not until November does the 120 day gestation period get underway. Each litter of young armadillos begins with a single fertilized egg. The armadillo always has four young and they are always identical, either all male or all female.

When the four identical young are born, usually in February, they are already miniatures of their parents, and able to walk around in a few hours. Their wild enemies include coyotes and bobcats, but greater danger comes from dogs around human population centers. Armadillos by the hundreds die on highways. The armadillo has a strange habit, when frightened, of leaping into the air, and vehicles that might have otherwise passed over them often strike and kill them instead.

Even faced with all of these threats, the armadillo prospers and has been extending its territory farther and farther inland.

The armadillo has poor vision and ineffective hearing but apparently has the ability to smell earthworms and other items of food at considerable depths as it roots along in the soft humus and leaf litter using its nose to uncover items of food.

In hunting, it alternately walks and trots, but if threatened, is capable of considerable speed hurrying back to the safety of its burrow.

Above: An armadillo in Florida.

Pronghorn

The pronghorn—also called antelope—lives wild only in North America, where it has an ancient ancestry. Today it is the only member of its family left. It is a westerner and its range has shrunk in historic times. Once, however, it occupied the open grasslands from central Texas and North Dakota into southern Canada, westward into Oregon and California and south deep into Mexico. Within this range, it lived in prairie communities with the bison, prairie dogs, coyotes and other creatures, relying on the grassland ecosystems for survival.

When Lewis and Clark first explored the west in 1805, there may have been thirty-five million pronghorns living in the vast open reaches of the continent. The pronghorns lifted their heads to watch the advancing party in the distance, then flashed warnings to others of their kind and dashed away at full-speed over the prairies. The restless animals keep watch over the countryside, and the slightest movement in the distance catches their attention. When a pronghorn runs to escape danger, others of the herd join in flight without questioning the nature of the hazard. Even the fawns a few days old are capable of reaching speeds in excess of 20 miles an hour. Adult pronghorns race across the prairies at 40 miles an hour or more. The antelope is the fastest land animal in North America.

They have strong legs, and they bound along, even over rocky ground, with a superlative surefootedness, neither stumbling nor slowing down. They sometimes leap through the air in outstanding broad jumps, covering 20 feet or more.

If the antelope is to run in this manner, it must use large quantities of oxygen. It is equipped with an especially large heart and lungs for its size, and with an over-sized windpipe. When it runs, its mouth drops open and large amounts of air are taken in to supply oxygen.

The pronghorn is beautifully colored, with reddish-brown above, pure white on the undersides and rump and large black and white markings on its head and neck.

Both male and female have permanent horns. These are small on the females, shorter usually than the animal's ears, but old males have horns 12 inches long or more. The forked horn gives the pronghorn its name. After the annual breeding season, the outer sheath of the horns falls off and is replaced.

Pronghorns show a preference for living together in herds that may include several hundred animals of all ages and sexes. As spring approaches, however, the herds begin to break up. The dominant males establish territories where they guard their bands of does, yearlings and fawns.

The males may be challenged by other males and engage in a series of face-offs and brief chases and perhaps even a fight. The dominant bucks, those of the greatest size and strength, succeed in fathering most of the new fawn crop.

Above: A young pronghorn.
Below: Pronghorns on the Montana plains.

The fawns are born in May or June, and there are usually twins. The doe hides her newborn young in the grass and sagebrush but they are precocious young and need not stay long in seclusion. Within a day or two, they are moving over the rolling plains, staying close to their mother, but always ready to dash off at top speed. At this age the young antelope is at its most vulnerable. They play as they grow and build strength and agility, bounding up and down and conducting sprinting contests.

Although the antelope is capable of high speed and distance running, it normally stays close to home. As long as food, whether green grass in summer or sagebrush, rabbitbrush and greasewood in other seasons, is abundant, the pronghorn stays within a three or four mile wide territory. It may, however, make seasonal migrations, especially down from the mountains in autumn to the valleys where winter snow is not so deep.

Even with its superior speed, the antelope is seldom safe from its predators. Coyotes cannot outrun the healthy individual, but are said to form relay teams to run by turns until the pronghorn can go no further. Bears, foxes and eagles are also numbered among the antelope's enemies.

The young face the greatest hazards. The golden eagle will take young fawns, if found away from the mother.

People, however, have been the most effective enemy of the pronghorn. White hunters took the pronghorns for meat. Ranchers built fences across their trails, and fences are the downfall of pronghorns. They do not leap over fences but crawl under them instead. Fences may catch and hold pronghorns until they starve.

Within half a century after the West was invaded by ranchers, the pronghorn was in jeopardy. They were rescued just in time. Strict hunting regulations and establishment of wildlife refuges helped them recover. Today they are once more secure.

Above: Pronghorns on the run.
Opposite: The graceful pronghorn, seen here on the prairies of Saskatchewan, is North America's fastest land animal.

America's Forests

Porcupine

The range of the porcupine extends across the northern part of North America from Newfoundland to Alaska. In the east it is found in the forests south through Pennsylvania, and in the west it lives as far south as Mexico.

It is a slow moving, heavy, short-legged rodent, clumsy in appearance and lumbering in gait. Of the total length of 25 to 35 inches, the tail accounts for seven to nine inches. The adult weighs between 10 and 28 pounds which would seem to make it a choice food item for a wide variety of predators. In truth, however, the porcupine is avoided by most animals capable of killing it, because its protective coat is among the most effective worn by any wild animal.

Spread across its back and tail are thousands of spiny quills, modified hairs with needle sharp points. If the point becomes imbedded in an enemy, the porcupine sheds the quills easily. They are, however, extremely difficult to extract from the victim's flesh. Dog owners use pliers to pull the quills from their pets and hunting dogs. If the quills are left imbedded, they work deeper and deeper into the animal's body and bring on complications that can kill it. Experienced dogs seldom attack porcupines. They know what to expect.

The attacker approaches and the porcupine wheels and turns its rump to its enemy. By backing into trouble, it keeps its tail foremost and the tail is the fastest moving part of a porcupine. The porcupine can flick it with remarkable speed and slap an attacking animal in the face.

The porcupine does not, as it is sometimes claimed, 'throw' quills at its enemies. Instead, once threatened, the animal, with its remarkable sense of touch, becomes an instant pincushion. A highly developed layer of muscle beneath the skin promptly

Opposite: A porcupine's quills, though once sought as ornamentation by American Indians, protect him from most predators. Below: A porcupine rests on a tree branch.

turns every quill into the attack position. Some predators, however, including fishers, foxes, coyotes and bobcats, have learned that they can flip the porcupine onto its back and kill it by slashing the unprotected belly.

Porcupines are vegetarians whose favorite food is the living cambium layer growing under the bark of trees. For this reason, orchardists trap porcupines, kill them with clubs, or shoot them whenever possible. Professional foresters have estimated that a single porcupine can cause thousands of dollars in damage to forest trees during its lifetime. In addition, porcupines sometimes attack vacation cabins that people have locked up for the winter, or they chew handles from axes and other hand tools to obtain the salt in them. Cabin owners commonly leave a block of salt outside in winter to lure the porcupines away from their cabins.

In a rocky ledge or pile of stones where she is protected from other animals, the female gives birth to a single young porcupine each year. The youngster is already fully developed at birth. It weighs perhaps one and a half pounds and has quills that, as soon as they are dry, are needle sharp and ready for action, a miniature copy of its parents. The young one stays with its mother for a few weeks and is soon feeding on succulent herbs. The mother pays less and less attention to it until the youngster wanders off through the woods alone.

Beaver

Among the wild creatures, the beaver is the supreme engineer, eagerly refashioning the landscape to fit its needs. It constructs dams and lodges and sometimes even builds canals that enable it to move food and building materials to where they are needed.

Running water challenges beavers, especially if it sounds like a leak in a dam they have built. So at night the male beaver repairs leaks in the dam, and if it is a big job, other members of the family may join in the task.

We may think of beavers as having superior intelligence, but they do not rate high on any intelligence scale. Much of their work, including the felling of trees, appears to be totally instinctive. The tree falls where gravity takes it, and if the beaver is working on a streambank, the slope usually causes the trees to fall into the water where the animals can make the best use of them.

A beaver, cutting a tree, sits up on its hind legs and gnaws away large chips all around the tree. When the tree falls, the beaver dashes off, usually in time to escape. But not always. Some beavers are caught by the trees they cut.

Although beavers normally cut small trees that are easily moved, they have been known to fell trees that measure more than five feet in diameter. They have also been guilty of dropping trees where they cause trouble for unwary people. A Missouri angler, floating on his favorite fishing stream, had his boat swamped by a falling tree. The boat was demolished, but the fisherman escaped. Beavers have even been known to drop trees across power lines, short out the wires and cause fires that burn down farm buildings.

This animal can also cause trouble with its dams. Beavers frequently dam up culverts, or build their dams so high they flood highways and croplands. When the dams are removed, the beavers may come back the following night to rebuild them.

For the most part, however, the beaver's association with people has been a happy one. This is the animal largely responsible for the opening of the Northwest. When white people first came to North America, beavers lived over much of the continent and their furs were important items of trade. As the beavers were killed off, trappers and traders moved deeper into the wilderness, following rivers and lakes into remote places where beavers were still found. Mountain men in search of beavers discovered new wonders, including the Yellowstone National Park.

The dense fur of the beaver protects the animal in frigid water as it swims beneath the ice on northern lakes and streams. The

Below, left and right: The beaver, North America's largest rodent, nibbles and gnaws on trees and twigs.

beaver spends much time combing its hair and keeping its coat in prime condition, using special claws on the two inner toes of its hind feet. These combs are used by the beaver for grooming and spreading its waterproofing oil over the fur.

The beaver's lodge is generally a conical pile of logs surrounded by water that becomes a moat to help keep predators at a distance. Before winter, the beaver stores up its food supply for the cold months when the northern landscape is locked in ice and snow. This food consists of lengths of green wood from which the family strips bark whenever hungry.

This wood-cutting can even be done underwater by the well-equipped beaver. Both the animal's nose and ears are outfitted with valves that close whenever the beaver submerges, then open again as it surfaces. Its lips can be closed behind its long, curving teeth, enabling the working beaver to cut wood underwater.

The beaver is North America's largest rodent. The average adult beaver weighs 40 pounds or more and there are records of individuals weighing more than 90 pounds. They continue to grow as long as they live and, in the wild, may live a dozen years or so.

Beaver mate for life and each spring the female gives birth to a new litter of three or four young. From the time of their birth, they are covered with fur and their eyes are open.

The young stay with their parents for two years. Usually the family occupying the lodge consists of the parents and their two latest litters of young. When the young ones are two years old, they are chased away from the family lodge to explore for mates and territories of their own.

As human pressure on the beavers built, their numbers fell until much of their original range had no beavers remaining. Ohio, for example, had lost all its beavers by 1830. One hundred years passed before they started to come back. The timberlands were returning and with the trees came the forest wildlife, including the beavers. Today this state has enough beavers to conduct an annual trapping season. What has happened in Ohio is a typical example of how the beaver has returned in recent decades to much of its former range.

Above: The beaver uses powerful teeth to cut down trees to build dams and elaborate waterways.
Below: The beaver's large flat tail is useful for packing the mud used as cement in the construction of his dams.

Wherever the beaver lives, its construction projects help other wildlife. Their dams conserve water and moose and deer come to the beaver pond to drink. Trout live in the ponds, and ducks nest there while kingfishers, mink, raccoons, turtles and others feed there.

Cottontail

Of all North American mammals the cottontail may be the best known and best loved. These popular animals prosper from coast to coast and from southern Canada southward across the continent. In appearance there is nothing particularly distinctive about a cottontail except for its oversized ears. It has a short powderpuff tail, of no apparent use, and long hind legs. It is covered with drab brownish gray fur that is low grade by our standards.

Enemies of the cottontail are legion. Hawks, owls, bobcats and coyotes will all catch and eat rabbits at every opportunity. So will foxes and dogs. In addition, rabbits must cope with disease and parasites while weather is a particularly serious hazard for very young rabbits still in the nest. Early litters are frequently lost to spring floods or exposure. In winter rabbits are less able to escape their predators through the snow.

To compensate for these constant drains, the cottontail, each spring, goes on a production campaign. The earliest mating comes late on a winter night when the adults meet and sometimes stage a hopping contest, a moonlight courtship dance.

Once the female has mated, however, the dancing ends and she may turn on her mate, tear mouthfuls of fur from him and drive him from her territory. Four weeks later she gives birth to her litter, usually four to six young.

The first step is to prepare a place for her family. She does this by using her front paws to dig a shallow bowl-shaped depression in the ground. Ordinarily her chosen homesite is in an open grassy field, but she may select a brushy covert or even a garden or yard. Once the depression is complete, the female lines this with grass and then with fur pulled from her underside.

Preceding page: A closeup of a cottontail.
Left: A cottontail rests in a hollow log.
Below: The snowshoe hare, a cousin of the cottontail, during his wintertime all-white phase.

By the time they are ten days to two weeks old they are furry little copies of their parents and are leaving the nest to find their own green foods. Their mother, who probably re-bred when the young were only days old, is already preparing to have her second litter. In this manner, the mature healthy female cottontail can produce four and sometimes five litters in the course of a summer breeding season that may continue for seven months.

Within its territory the rabbit knows well the secret hiding places into which it can dash to escape predators. These refuges are brush piles, thickets and burrows dug by other animals. In addition, the rabbit, when confronted by an enemy, is a surprisingly able combatant. Its hind feet, equipped with sharp claws, can inflict injury.

The newborn young weigh about an ounce each. They are naked and red and their eyes and ears tightly closed. They are fed on milk and within a week they are covered with fur and jostling each other in the nest. The female stays away from the nest most of the time and this serves to keep predators from finding the young easily.

The young are fed at night, when the mother's presence is least likely to give away the location. While the young are in the nest, they are helpless prey for crows, snakes, dogs, cats and weasels.

When the female rabbit leaves her infants, she pulls a fur blanket over them, then hides them beneath a leaf or two and a few blades of grass.

Gray Squirrel

The gray squirrel, North America's best known tree squirrel, is still a citizen of the forest, as it always has been. In the East it lives in the hardwood forests while the western gray squirrel is at home in the oaks and pines of western Oregon, Washington and California. But beyond the forest boundaries it has extended its list of suitable habitats to take advantage of new conditions created by human development because it possesses an innate adaptability to life in the trees of villages, cities and parks.

When eastern North America was still shaded by deep forests, the squirrels could, if they chose, travel for miles without descending to the ground. Settlers, who sometimes called the gray squirrel 'silvertail', fought hordes of squirrels that came to their fields to eat grain. There were even bounties placed on squirrels. Some years, the gray squirrels began moving by the millions in one direction until waves of them were advancing through the country, lemming style, even swimming rivers and lakes.

Then the timber cutters moved on the forests, the trees vanished and with them went the squirrels. By the first part of this century there was concern that the gray squirrel might become extinct. Gradually, however, the forests began to recover and with the return of the trees, squirrels, along with other forest wildlife, began to return also.

An adult gray squirrel weighs a pound and measures 10 inches long, in addition to an eight-inch tail. Gray squirrels are not always gray. Typically there is brown fur mixed with the gray and some populations are black. The underparts of the squirrel are white. Two times each year the gray squirrel changes its fur coat, losing the old hair gradually until the coat is

Below: Western gray squirrels are found in the Sierra Nevadas as well as in the coastal mountain ranges.
Opposite: A playful squirrel scampers down an ivy-clad California cypress.

replaced. It goes into the winter wearing a new coat of fur that locks in the insulating air and shuts out the cold. Grooming, by licking, plus occasional dust baths, keeps the coat in condition. There is no sexual color dimorphism. Males and females look alike.

The gray squirrel has no fear of high places. It dashes from limb to limb with breath-taking abandon, sometimes leaping through the air to a new perch, sometimes catching the very tip of a slender branch that dips low while the squirrel swings beneath it, running upside down until it scrambles onto the top of the limb. Squirrels playing tag in the trees race full speed up and around the trunks and through the branches. Even the most observant squirrel watchers rarely see a gray squirrel fall. On those rare occasions when this happens, the animal reaches out for every branch it passes and frequently catches one and rescues itself. Failing this, the squirrel hits the leafy forest floor feet first, shakes itself and scampers back up the tree unhurt.

One explanation for the squirrel's ability to climb rests in the long, curved nails on each of its toes, tree hooks that dig into bark easily. The long tail is also an aid; it whips from side to side, helping the squirrel maintain its balance.

In addition, gray squirrels have excellent vision and good depth perception. The placement of its eyes tell the squirrel what transpires all around it. It can see the skies overhead where the red-railed hawk soars and watch what goes on behind it without turning its head. Meanwhile it can watch the ground below.

The squirrel's hearing is excellent. When on the ground searching for food the female can hear the high pitched squeaking of her babies in the nest far above, and a walking hunter is heard at a distance.

The gray squirrel is also aided by an excellent sense of smell. In autumn it buries nuts in the ground and these are later located, not by memory, but by sniffing them out. In addition to nuts, the gray squirrel feeds on fruit plus the seeds of maple and other trees. In spring it eats the new buds of awakening trees. Squirrels have even been observed cutting the bark of maple trees in late winter to drink the sweet sap that runs from the wound. The adult gray squirrel needs about two pounds of food a week to stay healthy and active.

Females frequently give birth to two litters of young each year with the first family arriving at the end of winter or very early spring. The gestation period is forty days and typically the female gives birth to quadruplets. The newborn squirrel, naked, blind and helpless, weighs half an ounce and must gain both warmth and nourishment from its mother's body. Not until it is thirty-two days old do its eyes open.

The female gray squirrel is a fierce protector of her young and has been known on rare occasions to attack and bite people she believed threatened her nest. If discovered, she may also move her entire family to a different den.

Enemies of the gray squirrel have difficulty reaching them, but raccoons sometimes take the young ones from the nest, and so will snakes and opossums, while hawks and owls may capture adults. Generally, however, the gray squirrel is hard to catch and not a reliable source of food for predators.

Above: A pair of California gray squirrels chase one another around a tree.

Opposite, top: Eastern tree squirrels inhabit the hardwood forests of the Appalachian region.

Opposite, lower left: Red squirrels, like this one photographed in Montana, live in the Rocky Mountains.

Opposite, lower right: An eastern gray squirrel in Tennessee.

Woodchuck

The woodchuck's habit of feeding along roadsides or in open fields makes it a well known character in rural America. The range of this large member of the squirrel family covers the northeastern part of the continent from Oklahoma east to North Carolina, north into Canada and the Hudson Bay country, then west to eastern Alaska.

The woodchuck is seldom confused with any other animal. It is a large ground dwelling rodent with short legs and a short tail. The ears are small and the body is heavy. The fur of the woodchuck, which is of little value for human use, is coarse and has a brownish color sometimes tinged with gray or red. The adult measures from 18 inches to two feet in length, stands 6 or 7 inches high at the shoulder, and may weigh twelve pounds when ready to hibernate in the fall.

The woodchuck, or groundhog, is at home on the woodland borders, where there are open fields nearby to provide the living conditions needed. In former times, before the land was settled and farmed, woodchucks were less common than they are today. Then came farmers to cut the forests, plow the fields and maintain grasslands for their livestock. In the brushy fence rows, along the edges of the thickets and the creek banks, the woodchucks dug their burrows, while in the open fields they found the foods they needed, and the animal flourished.

The woodchuck, a member of the wildlife underground community, digs elaborate burrows which promise it safety in all seasons. The burrow may be 30 feet or more long and have a number of openings. The main entrance is characterized by the mound of earth which the animal kicks outdoors as it excavates its home. But there are other exits which have no mound of earth. When threatened by predators, as the woodchuck frequently is, it dashes for a plunge hole leading to its underground sanctuary. It may also use the plunge hole as an exit if predators come into its burrow.

The woodchuck is a true hibernating mammal. As winter comes on, it feeds heavily, storing up a layer of fat to provide the energy that will keep it going during the winter months. During those frigid weeks the woodchuck is deep underground. Hibernation for the woodchuck normally extends from November into late February or March—about ⅓ of the year. During this time the woodchuck's body processes slow down dramatically. The heart beat drops from 75 to four times a minute while the body temperature falls from 90°F to perhaps 38°F. Metabolism slows.

Scientists still do not understand all that happens when the woodchuck hibernates. They know that the woodchuck is much heavier in the fall, as it goes into its burrow for the winter, than it is in the spring when it awakens, thin and weak. During the winter it loses 30 to 40% of its fall weight. The woodchuck in hibernation coils into a ball and rests on its lower abdomen with its tail and hind parts wrapped over the head. As spring comes on, the woodchuck spends more time outdoors eating. It feeds in the daytime and sometimes stretches out in the sun to rest.

The breeding season begins soon after the animals come out of their winter quarters. Gestation lasts for 31 to 33 days, then, toward the end of March, the female gives birth to her annual litter of two to nine young. All are naked and blind, weighing about one ounce each.

By mid-summer, when the young woodchucks are about half grown, they begin to practice digging on burrows of their own near the family homestead and they are soon ready to leave home. Now they must take care of themselves and find new territories in which to live, and this is a time of peril for young woodchucks as they spread out over the countryside.

In addition to the pressure put on them by people who object to having their gardens destroyed and buildings undermined, the woodchuck is prey to foxes, eagles, coyotes and other predators. Young woodchucks are taken by a variety of hawks.

The burrows dug by and for woodchucks also serve the needs of various other wild neighbors, including snakes, skunks, rabbits, and even pheasants seeking refuge.

Top: A woodchuck perched in a tree.
Bottom: A young woodchuck.
Opposite: Traditionally, winter's duration is foretold by the woodchuck's seeing his shadow when he emerges from hibernation.

Raccoon

The raccoon is widely recognized by people, and is one of the most successful wild mammals in North America. Its range extends over most of the continent from Central America into southern Canada. In recent years it has been extending its range northward into Canada's prairie provinces.

The spreading of the raccoon's range has been made easier by its adaptability to the changes people brought to its world. The wild raccoon lives normally where there is a combination of large timber and water. Its tracks are often seen along woodland streams. The trees provide it denning sites in which to take refuge and raise its family. The streams provide much of its food.

Outside the forest, however, the raccoon has, in recent times, taken up residence in towns and cities. People are frequently awakened by its noisy midnight raids on garbage cans. Furthermore, the noise awakens dogs and sets them to barking throughout the neighborhood. Raccoons may even tip garbage cans over and roll them bumping and thumping down driveways in the darkness of night.

In addition, raccoons attract the attention of people by raiding their gardens. Fresh vegetables are choice fare, and sweet corn in the milk stage is a special favorite. Raccoons also invade chicken pens, thereby earning the animosity of farmers.

The color of the raccoon varies somewhat with the part of the range in which the individual lives. Generally, however, its coat is a grizzled grayish-brown with black mask-like markings around the face, and six or seven rings around the tail. The adult raccoon is a stocky muscular animal 30 to 36 inches long, stands a foot high at the shoulders and weighs 10 to 25 pounds, although much larger ones have been taken. Once a year it

Opposite: A raccoon is startled while feeding.
Below: A raccoon family.
Following page: A raccoon feeding in a stream.
Raccoons do not, as often believed, wash their food, but rather they simply prefer their food to be moist.

changes its coat, wearing a thinner, lighter summer fur, and changing again in late summer or early autumn to a heavy coat of dense fur. It is this winter coat that gives the raccoon its value to trappers.

One secret of the raccoon's success is the wide variety of food that it finds acceptable. Both animal and vegetable foods are on its diet. It is especially fond of crayfish, frogs, snakes and mollusks which it harvests from the streams flowing through its woodlands. But it is not adverse to eating mice, shrews, insects and earthworms. The raccoon also feeds on turtle eggs, bird eggs and young birds in the nest. It is sometimes considered an important factor in holding down populations of waterfowl and game birds.

In summer and fall, berries, nuts, and grains are regular additions to the raccoon diet. It will also eat acorns and nuts.

As autumn comes, the raccoon lays on an inch-thick layer of fat across the rump and back which provides energy during the long, lean winter months when food may be scarce and storms may keep the animal holed up in the den for days at a time. There it sleeps but does not hibernate. It awakens easily in time of danger. By late February or March, throughout much of their range, the males are out searching for mates. Raccoon tracks are seen in the snow and along muddy creek banks. The males are polygamists and after the breeding season, pay little or no attention to any of their families. The young are born in April or May after a gestation period of 63 days. The average litter has four young but the number may vary from three to seven. For the next eight or ten weeks the young remain in the mother's den to be fed on milk. Thereafter, they join the mother on her nightly hunting trips and begin to learn the ways of survival for wild raccoons.

Throughout the summer and the coming winter the young stay with their mother, living in the family den. The following spring, however, the family breaks up. The young must now go out seeking new territories of their own. By this time the females among the young are most likely pregnant and ready to start families of their own.

The raccoon does not, as is sometimes suggested, wash everything it eats. It is doubtful that its habit of dipping food into water has anything to do with cleanliness. It is instead only an indication that raccoons prefer moist food.

Opposite and below left: Raccoons are often found scavenging near houses.

Below right, top: A young raccoon splashes playfully in a fountain.

Below right, bottom: A pair of young raccoons look through a hole in a fence.

Striped Skunk

This cat-sized mammal is native to much of North America from Mexico northward deep into Canada. It is generally black with a pair of wide, white bands that extend up the back and join on top of the head. The skunk's hair is long and its tail long and bushy. The head is shaped like a triangle and the nose is pointed. There is wide variation in the proportions of black and white fur from individual to individual.

The feature for which skunks are famous is the pair of pea-sized anal glands from which they can secrete, often with stunning accuracy, a chemical substance with an odor so strong that it may cause nausea. This is the skunk's major weapon. When attacked or threatened, the skunk turns its tail toward the enemy and stamps its feet. If this warning fails, it releases the liquid, often scoring a direct hit in the eyes of the attacker. Even young skunks are equipped to mount this chemical offensive. Replenishing the supply may require several days, however, and skunks do not expend their odorous liquid without serious provocation.

A variety of foods is acceptable to the striped skunk. One study of 1700 skunk stomachs, found that 57 percent of the animals' food was insects, 18 percent fruit, 10 percent animal matter and 2 percent birds and eggs. In spring, skunks prey heavily on mice. Individuals may also invade the farmer's hen-house to steal eggs. Skunks do their hunting at night, poking leisurely along fencerows and field borders wherever the lure of food takes them. Their search may last throughout the night, and daylight may find them a considerable distance from their favorite den, in which case the skunk simply searches out a suitable alternate hiding place for the day. There may or may not already be skunks present, but these animals seem not to object to the company of others of their kind.

When winter comes, skunks sometimes stay in their underground dens for long periods, sleeping through the storms, curled up in a leafy nest at the end of their burrow for days on end. They do not hibernate.

The young are born in April and May and usually there are four or five to the litter. When they are still quite small, the

female may lead them away from the family den on brief evening hunts; they follow her, walking in a line, along the fence row or the border of the woodland.

By the time the young are two months old and the end of summer is approaching, they leave their mother and wander off on their own, searching out territories for the coming winter.

North American skunks also include the hog-nosed skunk and the spotted skunk. The spotted skunk is a small species found over much of the southern part of the United States and south into Central America. The hog-nosed skunk, which has a naked snout that accounts for its name, is found in Mexico and southward throughout much of South America, but also lives in parts of Texas, Colorado and Arizona.

Above: A pair of young skunks scamper playfully after their nearby mother.
Opposite: A striped skunk, in Canada's Grasslands National Park, brandishes his tail.

Mink

The mink, a slender swift-footed member of the weasel clan, is found over most of the United States and Canada and everywhere is known for the beauty of its soft durable fur. The protective fur of the mink is dense underneath and covered with long shiny guard hairs that plaster down snugly when the animal goes into the water—as it often does.

But the beauty of its fur has also spelled trouble for the mink; trappers pursue it relentlessly to provide furs for the market. More than a century ago people began keeping mink in pens and raising them for their fur. Today this is a big industry and mink ranchers in the United States send more than four million of these pen-raised mink furs to market every year. Although mink can be kept in pens, they cannot be tamed. This creature is so wild of spirit that it refuses to adapt to the life of a pet.

An adult mink is about two feet long. One-third of this is tail. The male weighs from 1½ to 2½ pounds and the female is about 25 per cent lighter. This long slender hunter can slip through cracks and crevices of rocky streambank ledges, hollow logs and brushpiles. Because it is so active it burns energy rapidly and must eat often. It is an excellent hunter on land or in the water and underwater can outswim fish or slip up on an unwary duck, catch it by the foot and drag it under.

Mink concentrate their hunting along waterways where they take food of wide variety. Mink that live along seacoasts search the shores for clams and crabs. In the marshes they find fish, small birds and rodents. Farther inland they hunt along rivers, streams, lakes and ponds, where a meal for a mink may include fish, crayfish, rats, birds, frogs, snakes, salamanders, chipmunks and ducks. They store up food in times of surplus, and one naturalist found a mink's home supplied with 13 dead muskrats, two mallards and a coot.

The mink, a deadly enemy of the muskrat, will invade the muskrat's home when the rat is away and kill all the young muskrats. In addition, the mink may enter hen houses and, like other members of the weasel family, kill more than it can eat.

This is a solitary animal except in those brief periods of the year when males and females meet for mating. In this season, late in February or early in March, male mink, if they encounter each other in pursuit of the same female, may stage deadly fights. When excited or threatened the mink exudes a strong natural musk that is nauseating to some people. Unlike the skunk, however, the mink is incapable of directing a stream of this liquid at an enemy.

After mating, males and females split up. The male once again becomes a loner, traveling and hunting his territory in solitary fashion until the next mating season arrives. All care of the young falls to the female.

She chooses a hollow tree that has fallen, or pirates a den from some burrowing animal, and in this sanctuary, gives birth to five or six young. These infants have little resemblance to their parents; they have no fur and their eyes are closed. Within five weeks or so the young have opened their eyes and been weaned from their diet of milk. They spend the rest of the summer traveling with their mother on her hunting trips.

As summer disappears, the mink family breaks up. By autumn each of them has gone its own way, searching out individual territories along the waterways.

Mink have few natural enemies. Whether because of their speed, their willingness to fight, or their musk glands, other wild hunters prefer to leave them alone. Only the fox, lynx, snowy owl and great horned owl are serious natural enemies of this sleek and elusive animal.

Above: Mink concentrate their hunting along waterways.

Opossum

The opossum is a cat-sized animal with a long, narrow snout, beady dark eyes and a naked scaly tail. Its long coarse hair is mostly gray and of only limited commercial value. The opossum lives throughout most of the eastern part of the United States and northward into southern Canada. It is also found along the Pacific Coast where it was introduced. In recent years, the opossum has been expanding its range.

This animal is a marsupial that has changed little over millions of years. It carries its underdeveloped newborn young in a fur-lined abdominal pouch. The mating season comes in midwinter—January or February—and gestation lasts only 12 to 13 days. Usually the tiny young are so numerous that they cannot all survive. First they must make their way upward through the mother's fur toward the pouch, a trip of a few inches but one of the more remarkable and hazardous journeys in the animal world. The tiny, blind, naked opossums, embryo-like in most features, are but four-tenths of an inch long and weigh only .13 grams. The number that can survive is limited to 13 because the female has only 13 teats. After finding its way into the pouch the newborn infant must secure itself to a teat and there it stays until it is about two months old, when it is nearly as large as a house mouse.

Even after that, the young return to the nipple for food until they are 75 or 80 days old. Once the litter has outgrown the space in the mother's pouch, it travels with her, often riding on her back. The female may have two litters a year.

The opossum is strictly a nocturnal animal, spending its days hidden away in a hollow tree or log where it makes a nest of dry leaves gathered from the forest floor. Pushing the leaves beneath itself back toward the tail, the opossum gathers a whole roll of the bedding material into a bundle and carries it home to make a nest in which it sleeps.

The foods of the opossum are many and varied. Ninety percent by volume may be animal matter, crickets, ants, grasshoppers, wild birds and their eggs as well as mice, moles, young rabbits and, on occasion, eggs and chickens from the farmer's flock are eaten. They also kill crayfish, snakes, snails and frogs. Fruits, berries and other vegetable matter are eaten as well. The opossum is a garbage eater, frequently upsetting garbage cans in the middle of the night, and also finds carrion quite acceptable.

Among the strange qualities of this unusual animal is its tendency to play dead when confronted with danger. Scientists once believed this to be a willful act on the part of the opossum but more recent investigation indicates that the opossum may have little control over its death-like trance. The threatened opossum falls onto its side with eyes closed and tongue hanging from its mouth and no amount of abuse will make it move. During this time the heartbeat slows and the opossum seems to have fainted away. This inactivity doubtless saves it from many a predator which ceases its attack when the prey stops moving.

Automobiles are a major enemy of opossums that walk the highways at night, seldom hurrying and looking neither to right nor left. But the opossum remains abundant and enough escape the dogs, people and automobiles to ensure their continued prosperity in their varied ecosystems.

In recent times the opossum has been advancing into new territory in and around centers of human population. It has extended its range both to the north and west. Occasionally it can be found prospering in the center of our largest cities.

Top: The opossum, in recent years, has expanded his range to urban as well as rural areas.
Right: An opossum rests in a tree.

Fox

Foxes, smallest of North America's wild canids, resemble small dogs. The two most abundant species, the red fox and gray fox, are similar in size and general conformation. Both are elusive creatures that frequently live closer to our homes, even in the cities, than we realize.

The red fox, slightly larger than the gray, wears a rich, golden-reddish fur, has black feet and legs, and a white tip on its tail. The gray fox also has a reddish cast to the fur, especially on the ears, neck and legs, but overall it wears a basic grizzled gray coat.

Both have pointed faces with sharp noses, large erect pointed ears, and long bushy tails that serve as a counter-balance as the running fox turns swiftly from side to side, changing directions to pursue food or escape enemies. The luxurious, thick coat of the red fox is more valuable on the fur market than is that of the gray fox.

Together foxes live over most of North America and their ranges overlap in much of the United States. The range of the red fox extends from northern Alaska south almost to the Gulf coast. The gray fox lives over much of the United States and southward throughout central America. Within these ranges both prosper where there is a mixture of woodlands and open fields, streams, thickets, and wastelands where they can find food and live in relative safety from people and other enemies.

The red fox is the favorite of hunters and those who ride to the hounds because this nimble quick-witted animal challenges and confuses the hounds and keeps the chase going sometimes for hours. Unmounted hunters sitting on a hilltop on an autumn

Above: A young gray fox.
Opposite and following page: A young fox in its den.

Above & opposite: A red fox amid autumn colors on Isle Royale in Lake Superior.

night follow the progress of their fox hounds from hill to hill. The fox doubles back on its trail, slips across creeks on fallen logs, runs along the tops of stone or rail fences, all of which serve to confuse its pursuers. The gray fox, however, when pursued, seeks shelter quickly in a den or hollow log. The gray fox has one other possible escape route: it can climb trees, especially if there are low limbs onto which it can leap.

Natural enemies of the foxes include wolves, coyotes, lynxes, and bobcats, plus parasites and disease. As the young foxes emerge from the home den and begin moving around the territory they are also in danger from the great horned owl.

Foxes are primarily, but not exclusively, flesh eaters. Rodents are choice fare and so are rabbits and any other small mammals they can capture. Bird eggs and young are taken, while insects, both adult and larvae, are also eaten. Carrion is acceptable. Furthermore, as farmers frequently learn, foxes may take domestic fowl. Feathers and chicken bones are often found around fox dens, but there is a possibility that the fox picked up a chicken or its parts from a road or dump and is condemned on the basis of circumstantial evidence. Foxes also eat fruit.

Raising the fox family demands the attention of both male and female. Mating time for the red fox comes in February or earlier in the South. The female may return year after year to the same den. The red fox den, which may in the beginning have been excavated by a woodchuck, will normally have several entrances.

Fifty-three days after the red foxes mate, the female gives birth to her young, usually five or six of them, although the number may range from two to 10. Their eyes remain closed until they are nine days old. After a few weeks they begin to come out into the sunshine and play around the entrance of the family den, while the old foxes keep careful watch over them. The pups are about two months old when weaned, and by the time they reach the age of six months they are ready to leave the family.

Both red and gray foxes do most of their hunting at night and spend the daylight hours resting and hiding, although the red fox is more inclined to be abroad in daylight than is the gray fox.

The homesite chosen by the gray fox may be a hollow log, or a protected spot in a thick brush pile or rocky area. Or it may be a burrow. Here the fox makes a bed of leaves and grass and 51 days after mating gives birth to her litter, usually three to five young, that are blind when born, and nearly naked. The father helps bring food to feed the pups. The young gray foxes are ready for their first hunting lessons when three months old, but the family stays together into autumn when the young foxes are nearly as large as their parents.

Foxes are resourceful members of the North American wildlife community, and overall are no big threat to the interest of people. Surely the outdoors would be less interesting without these little wild dogs, chasing through the fields and thickets and yapping to each other in the darkness of night.

Opposite: A red fox stands over a rabbit that it has killed.
Below: A pair of young red foxes.

Black Bear

The range of the black bear covers much of North America, extending from central Mexico to the Arctic slope and from coast to coast. Within this broad expanse it is both loved and feared.

The black bear is a forest dweller by nature and it prefers to stay out of sight of people. For this reason, even where the bears survive today, they are seldom seen. They normally come out at night to feed, then spend the daylight hours in some secluded shelter. On occasion, they learn to raid refuse dumps where they are seen by people. More often, the only indicators of the bear's passing are the tracks it leaves in mud and sand, tracks resembling those of a barefoot boy except that the bear's foot is considerably wider than the human foot and shows claw marks.

Owners of northwoods cabins sometimes find that they have suffered visits by bears while their cabins are closed for winter. The bear may rip off shutters or doors and invade the cabin to search for food. Once inside, it can destroy cans of food, break glass containers, tear down shelves and upset furniture, leaving the place in a shambles.

Bears are also noted for their raids on beehives. The lure of honey seems irresistible to them. On occasion, big bears have killed livestock, especially pigs. For the most part, however, black bears stay in the woods out of sight and out of trouble. If they show up in a settlement, they risk being shot at or run down by dogs.

On the American frontier, bears were frequently an important source of food. The bears disappeared from much of their original range as the shooting continued and the forests were cut, vanishing completely from states where they once lived in abundance.

More recently the forests have come back and so, in some places, have the bears. Reports of bear sightings occur with increasing frequency.

Most people would recognize a black bear instantly. When full-grown, it is four to six and a half feet long and stands about three feet high at the shoulders. It weighs 200 to 300 pounds although rare large ones have weighed 500 pounds or more. Unlike the grizzly, the black bear has no hump on the shoulders and the face is not dished.

Its color is black or nearly so, as the name implies, but there are variations and exceptions. Black bears can come in three color phases: black, cinnamon, and tan. All three are seen in some regions including Yellowstone National Park, where a female may give birth to triplets of three different colors.

The bear walks flat-footed, swinging along from side to side. Its toes are equipped with short, curved claws which enable it to climb trees.

Below: A black bear at rest in Great Smoky Mountains National Park appears almost playful.

The black bear, like people, is omnivorous and what it eats depends largely on what is available. The list of acceptable bear foods includes insects, mammals, fish, reptiles and amphibians, alive or dead, as well as berries, roots, twigs, grass, fruit and nuts.

As winter approaches, black bears search out shelters for the cold months ahead. Often their winter den is a space hollowed out beneath the roots of a tree or in a tangle of brush and rocks where they are protected. Then, as cold weather arrives, the bear settles into a deep sleep. This slumber is something less than true hibernation. The bear may come from its bed on occasion, especially in warmer regions, but in winter when food is normally scarce, the animal is capable of sleeping for weeks at a time.

In the middle of winter the female gives birth to her cubs. Often there are twins or triplets and they are exceedingly small when born. They are also blind, hairless, toothless, completely helpless creatures that must be nourished by the mother's milk through the winter months.

By spring, the cubs are ready to leave the den and travel with their mother. They have much to learn, and perhaps the most important thing is to recognize enemies. They soon learn that their mother means business when she grunts, telling them to take refuge in the nearest tree. If they fail to respond quickly, she may swat them with a broad paw.

The cubs play vigorously, sharpening their reactions and building their strength as they wrestle and race. They stay with their mother through the following winter. Females begin breeding when about three years old and have a new litter of young every second year. Their productive life is generally 10 to 12 years.

Adult black bears are seldom threatened by other wild animals. Where they share the range, grizzly bears and cougars are the black bear's enemies. Elsewhere, there are few wild animals that will attack an adult black bear. The black bear is the largest carnivore through much of its range and formidable in a fight. One animal, much smaller, that can cause it harm and sometimes death, is the porcupine. Major threats to the black bears, young or old, are habitat destruction, people and their dogs.

Perhaps people should be more tolerant of the black bear even when it upsets beehives and wrecks vacation cabins. 'Bears were here first,' we are reminded by one California wildlife biologist, 'and we invaded their living areas.'

Top: A black bear in cinnamon phase.
Middle: A black bear in black phase.
Bottom: A bear cub scratches his chin.

Whitetail Deer

The grace and beauty of the whitetail deer makes it everyone's favorite among North America's large animals. To see this deer slipping silently through the thickets, or standing, head high and fully alert, in the farmer's pasture sniffing the evening air for signs of danger, is an unforgettable outdoor experience. And, happily, the numbers of whitetail deer are increasing today. Some biologists believe that more whitetails stalk the face of North America today than ever before.

This deer, a gift of the forest, was vitally important to early settlers carving homes and farms from the wilderness. Venison was a favored food and deer skins were tanned and sewed into clothing while surplus skins were taken to market for barter and sale.

The pace of market hunting intensified and at the same time the forests disappeared. Deer numbers fell drastically until the animals became rare over much of their range and hunting was halted in many states. Before the beginning of this century some states that once had abundant deer no longer had a single one of these animals.

Then the picture began to change. The whitetail deer appeared again and as their numbers increased year by year, carefully planned hunting seasons were opened under professional supervision and the whitetail populations continued to grow.

Today the whitetail prospers in the landscape as people have altered it. Instead of unbroken forests stretching on mile after mile, the world of trees is broken into patterns of farms and villages. There is variety in the vegetation, abundant browse in the woods, especially along the edges of fields and forests.

Meanwhile, the deer are no longer faced with as many of their large natural predators as once lived here. The cougars are rare. Predation today comes from hunters, poachers and wild-running dogs. Even these, however, seem not to hold the deer populations down. More people see deer now than ever before.

The deer are so abundant that, on occasion, they become pests. There are frequent complaints that deer are eating from gardens and the heart-shaped footprints they leave behind identify them. What they do not ruin by biting and pulling off, they sometimes trample.

Even in villages, the deer can, and do, get into frequent trouble with people. They damage shrubs, flowers and gardens and sometimes disrupt traffic. In one city a young whitetail buck

Opposite: A four-point buck deer.
Below: A five-point mule deer buck.
Following page: A big five-point buck in Montana's Glacier National Park looks up from grazing.

Opposite: A mule deer doe in Yosemite National Park.
Above: A four-point buck with antlers in velvet in the Wasatch Rocky Mountains of Utah.

Pages 130 through 133: A newborn fawn is licked by his mother, then rises to take his first wobbly steps.

Following page: Four whitetails in eastern Montana.

Above: A herd of whitetail deer on the eastern Montana plains in late winter.

found his way into the residential section where he became confused. Children and dogs chased and surrounded him and eventually he was tied up and hauled off to the zoo. On highways, deer are a hazard to nighttime drivers. And a deer-car collision can cause serious damage to the automobile and sometimes its occupants.

How large the whitetail may grow depends on where it lives. They are at home from southern Canada to the Florida Keys. The smallest live in the south. The tiny key deer is a diminutive whitetail scarcely larger than a collie dog. The adult key deer buck may weigh 60 pounds, contrasting with its giant cousin in northern states where big bucks may weigh 300.

In winter, the deer wear a gray-colored fur that is long and thick enough to trap air and conserve body heat. For summer the fur changes to a lighter weight that is shorter and reddish in color.

Life for a whitetail fawn usually begins early in summer when the weather is pleasant and there is abundant food for the new mother. The doe, or female, commonly has twin fawns which she hides in thick, brushy places. The fawns, which have coats heavily spotted with white, lie in hiding, perfectly still if there is any threat of danger. On the sun-dappled forest floor they are camouflaged. Furthermore, they lack, at this age, the distinctive deer odor which later in life will be easily detected by dogs or wild canines.

By the time the fawns are four or five weeks old, they follow their mother at night as she feeds. Fawns may stay with the female through the first winter, learning the signs of danger and the rewards of wariness.

Deer are vegetarians but they eat a variety of plants. Leaves, twigs, acorns, grass, and flowers are all consumed as are mushrooms and fruit.

In spring the buck begins to grow his annual set of antlers which start as knobs on his head and enlarge rapidly during the summer. By late summer the new antlers have their full size and the layer of skin that covered their surface withers and falls away, leaving them bone hard.

In autumn, as the mating season approaches, the buck travels more in pursuit of the females or fights frequently with other bucks met along the trails. Then, after the rut is over, the buck's fine antlers become loose and fall off.

Now the bucks and does and the young deer too, may stay together into the winter. When winter foods become scarce and the weaker deer perish, others live out the winter and once more come into the spring and the season of rebuilding their numbers.

Opposite: A mule deer doe in Yosemite National Park.
Above: A pair of whitetails at sunset.

Wetlands And The Coasts

Sea Lion

Sea lions, along with fur seals, belong to the family of marine animals known as eared seals. There are two species of sea lions, the Steller's sea lion, a giant animal living from Alaska's Bering Straits south to southern California, and the smaller California sea lion. A large male Steller's sea lion may weigh a ton and measure 13 feet long, while his mates weigh considerably less. The male California sea lion weighs about half as much as the Steller's.

Of all the marine mammals, the sea lions may be the most widely known because trained seals used in circus acts are usually female California sea lions, gentle, intelligent and responsive to their trainers.

Unlike the fur seals, the sea lions wear coats that are coarse and of little commercial value. This has worked to their advantage. But the sea lion's eating habits have earned them condemnation from commercial fishermen for many decades. Sea lions live on fish, and fishermen frequently assume that these fish are species of high market value. Scientific studies, however, show that the sea lions normally eat less valuable fish, although they sometimes consume salmon.

Sea lions return, year after year, to their same rocky breeding grounds. For the California sea lions this is often on islands, from the Channel Islands southward to Mexico. Breeding colonies of Steller's sea lions are found through much of the animal's range, predominantly north of central California.

In spring, the males arrive first in the rookeries and promptly engage in combat with other males, contesting the boundaries of their territories until the weaker sub-dominant males are forced to give up hope of breeding for the season.

Next come the females, ready to give birth to their pups, swimming through the waves toward their natal islands. The rocky shores become crowded with large noisy animals, lumbering clumsily about on their flippers, fighting and squawling. Within a breeding male's harem there are usually 10 to 20 females. At birth the newborn young Steller's sea lion weighs 35 to

Opposite, top and bottom: Steller's sea lions on the rocky Alaskan coast.
Below: A harbor seal at Muir Inlet, Glacier Bay National Monument, Alaska.

50 pounds and is about 40 inches long. The young of the California species are somewhat smaller. At first, male and female pups are much the same size but in time, the males grow larger than the females.

While the adult females are in their rookeries, the males tend to stay home guarding their harems against raiders. California sea lion males may refuse to go to sea for food for as long as two months, but the male Steller's sea lion resists hunger less rigidly and goes off to feed more often.

Meanwhile the female goes to sea frequently to replenish her strength on squid and fish. She may be gone two or three days before finding her way back to the nursery. When she arrives, she goes straightaway to her own young pup, locating it, by some method not well understood, from the mass of seemingly identical pups.

The sea lion, regardless of its natural skills in the water, must learn to swim while still young. By the time it is two months old it is exploring the surf and soon, on the surface or underwater, is an expert swimmer capable of capturing its own food.

Late summer and early autumn is a time for rebuilding strength. The sea lions move off to sea, leaving their native islands until the following spring.

Their natural enemies while at sea include primarily the sharks and the killer whales. Even before white explorers arrived along the Pacific Coast of North America, these animals were being killed by native people. The hides of the Steller's sea lion were used for boat coverings while intestines were sewed into material for making raincoats. The meat was eaten and the oil was stored and used or bartered.

The sea lions today are more rigidly protected than ever before. As a result their populations appear to have stabilized and the barking and grunting of the sea lions promises to remain a memorable part of the wild scene along the Pacific coast and its offshore islands from California northward to the Bering Sea.

Seal

There are 32 species of seals around the world, all of them large mammals that make their homes in the oceans. They are divided into two families. One group, the eared seals, is made up of the fur seal and the sea lion. The much larger family contains all the other species, the true seals. Seals are predatory animals and fish are their major food item.

Among the best known of North America seals is the fur seal which makes its home on and around the Pribilof Islands in the Bering Sea. The males of this medium-sized species are usually six feet long and weigh 300 to 500 pounds. The females are noticeably smaller. The coat of the fur seal is mostly black, and their thick, silky fur is covered with coarse guard hairs.

The fur seals of Alaska have been in trouble since the earliest Russian explorers discovered them in 1786. Scientists believe that there may once have been as many as four million of these seals living on the Pribilofs, and these remote islands remain the home of the world's largest fur seal population.

At the end of summer, these seals slip into the dark water, leave their native islands and head out to sea for the winter. The females and young make longer trips than the males, but by the following spring all of them are heading back for the Pribilofs.

Right: A California sea lion stretches his neck amid a sleeping group including seals and elephant seals.

First come the old males, heavy, temperamental creatures. The strongest of them establish breeding territories along the dark, rocky beaches and are ready when the females arrive. The males begin at once herding females into their own territories. Within a few days each male has built up his harem, perhaps 40 or more females. For the next two months the male is so busy guarding his harem from other males that he cannot leave the beach even to feed.

Shortly after the females return, they give birth to their new pups, small, furry, black creatures, and within days mate again in preparation for the following year's new cycle of life.

Unlike the males, the females leave the nurseries to go off and feed. They may range 60 miles or more from the island in search of food and be gone for five days or more. During that time the infants must wait because each female accepts only her own pup to nurse. During this long wait, the young seals crowd together in nurseries where they spend much of their time sleeping. To the human ear their voices sound all alike, but the returning female can, through some series of signals that remain a mystery, pick her pup from the crowd.

They learn to swim when six to eight weeks old, and now must also begin learning how to harvest their own food from the ocean. By autumn the young of the year are strong enough to leave the island on their maiden voyage. During their long winter at sea, the young seals must provide for themselves and it is during this difficult time that many of them perish. Those that survive this test may live for as long as 20 years.

In their annual migrations, the females travel considerably farther than the males, sometimes thousands of miles along the coast as far south as California, then back, mysteriously guided by navigation systems which we do not fully understand. The travels of the Pribilof Island fur seals remain one of the truly outstanding accomplishments of migrating animals.

The fur seal once came dangerously close to extinction because many nations hunted them upon the open seas. Many of the seals killed were not recovered but sank into the water instead. In 1911, when the populations were dangerously low, the five major nations taking fur seals, the United States, Russia, Japan, Sweden and Denmark, signed a treaty that ended the killing of seals on the open oceans. As a result the seals are killed only on the Pribilofs, and there the annual harvest comes

Below: A harbor seal suns himself on a slab of ice in Alaska.
Left: California Sea Lions on the Farallon Islands off the California coast.
Following page: An elephant seal close up.

exclusively from the three-year old males which are not yet part of the breeding population. These skins are sold on the market and the treaty nations share the income. The Alaskan fur seal herd now numbers about one and a half million animals. Scientists monitor it carefully and must manage the kill to keep the herd at a safe level.

Elephant Seal

The elephant seal, one of the true, or earless seals, is the largest of all its clan. Its hind flippers turn backwards and propel it through the water. There are two types of elephant seals in the world, the southern one lives in the Antarctic and is the larger of the two. The northern elephant seal occupies the coastal islands of southern California and Baja California.

This northern elephant seal may be 15 feet long and weigh as much as 5000 pounds. They are yellowish or gray in color. The female is considerably smaller. The male seal has a long snout which can be inflated and which helps account for its name. Ordinarily this flabby snout hangs loosely on the front of the elephant seal's face.

The usual food of this animal is small fish. When cruising about under water in search of food the elephant seal can stay submerged for five minutes or longer which is possible, in part because of valves that shut water out of the nostrils.

When the time comes for the females to give birth to their young ones, usually between February and June, they seek out a stretch of beach away from the males whose clumsy movements and massive bodies would be a definite threat to the infant seals.

People have been the major enemy of the elephant seal. In the past, whalers invaded the beaches and killed the giant seals by the thousands for food and oil. As the herds of elephant seals became increasingly scarce government officials and conservationists were concerned for their welfare. In 1911, the Mexican government passed rules forbidding the taking of elephant seals and this was a major step in protecting the species. Among the natural enemies, the killer whale is the biggest threat.

Above: A sea-lion herd in Alaska.
Right: A female elephant seal suns herself on the California coast.

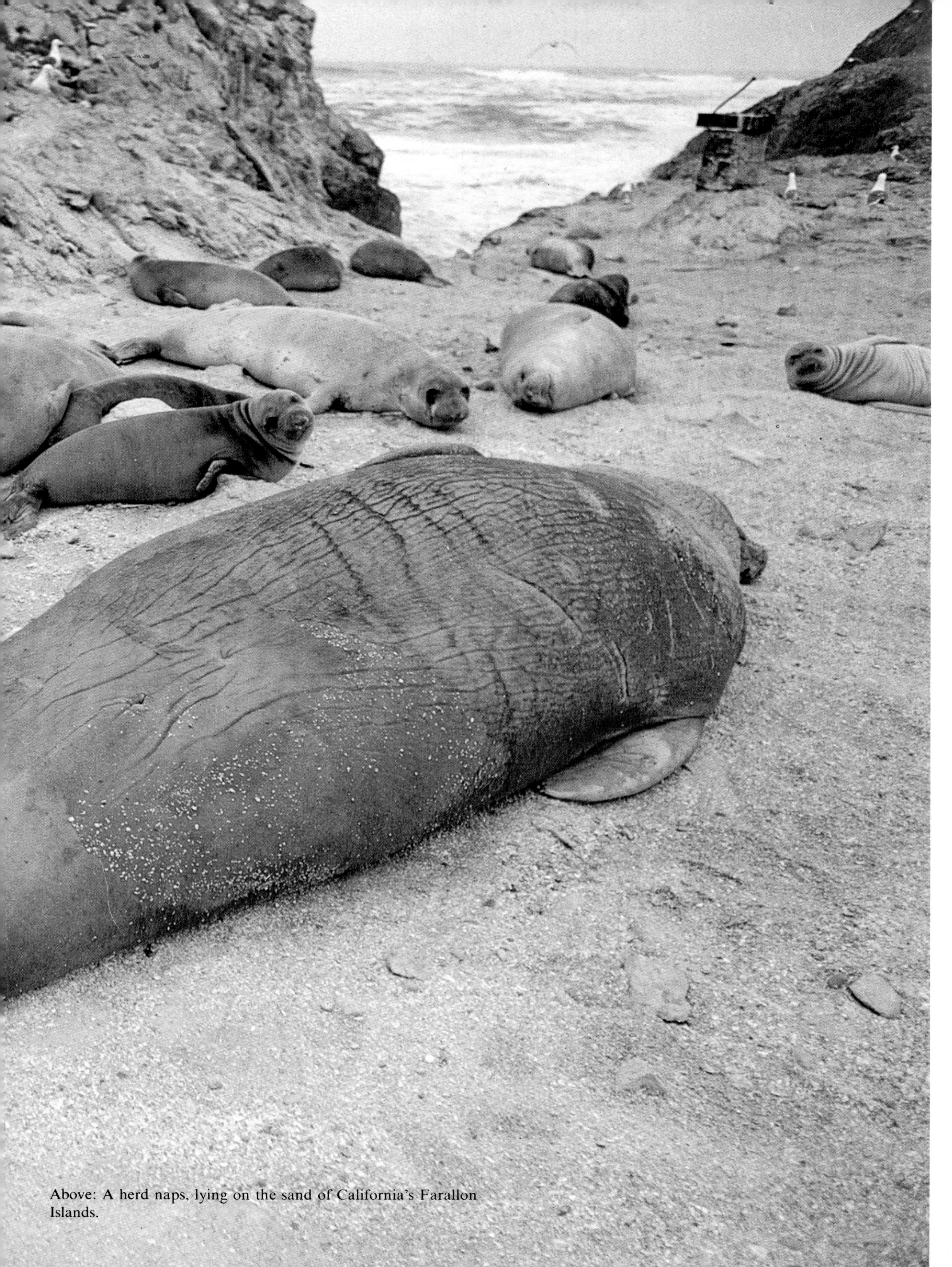

Above: A herd naps, lying on the sand of California's Farallon Islands.

Top: A male elephant seal dozes; Bottom: A female elephant seal nurses her pup.

Above: A pup scooting across the sand.

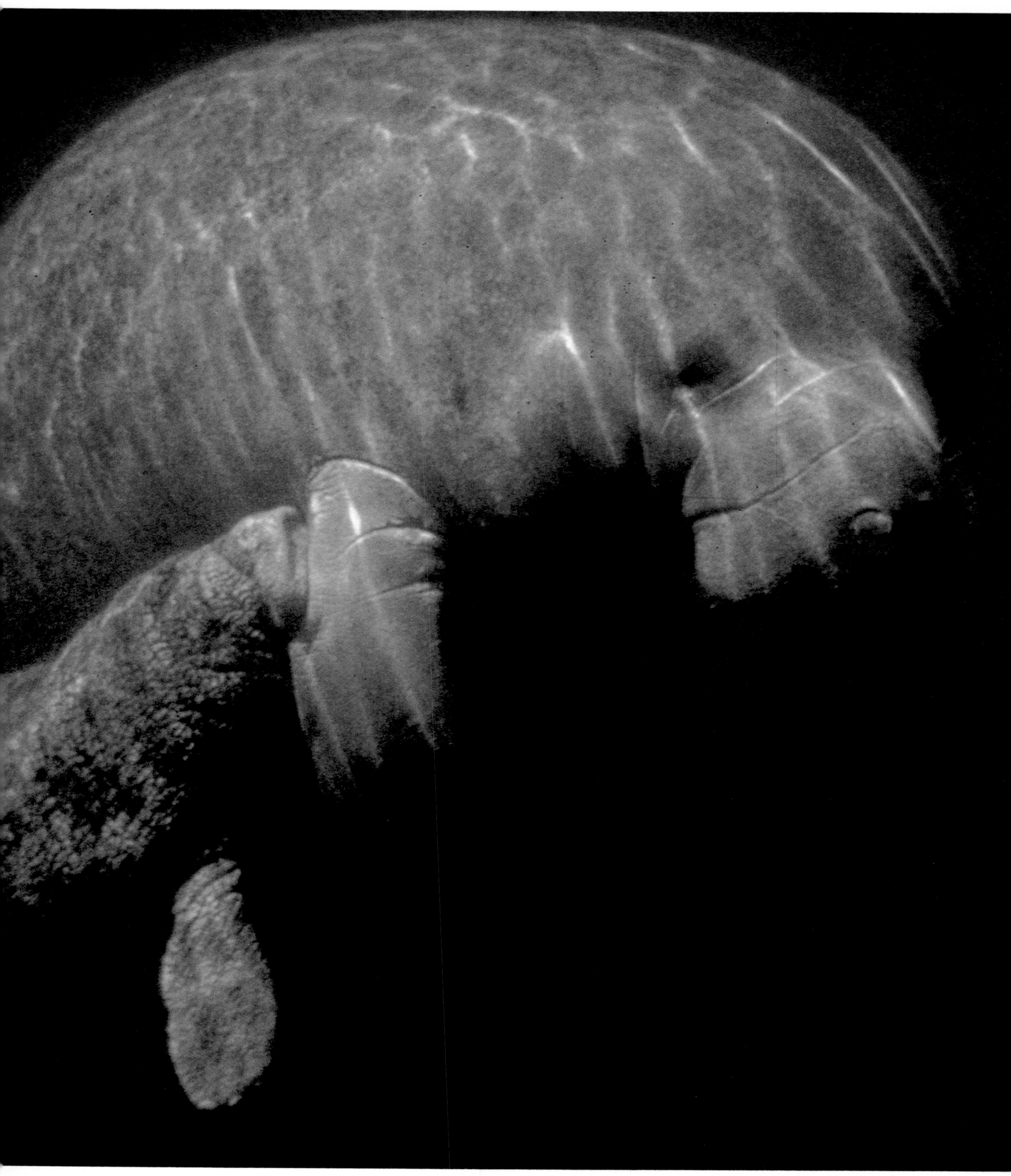

Manatee

The Manatee, the strange shapeless mammal of the order *Sirenia,* is among the most astounding animals that inhabit saltwater. The largest of all of them was discovered in 1841, in the Bering Sea. Known as Steller's sea cow, this giant, blubbery mammal, now extinct, measured 25 feet in length. A smaller cousin survives today, in greatly reduced numbers, along parts of the Florida coast. This endangered animal, the Florida sea cow, or manatee, weighs 1,000 pounds and has no hind limbs. The forelimbs are modified as flippers and the tail is a rounded fluke. The manatee is shapeless and lumpy. The skin is rough and gray. It has a broad muzzle and a flabby upper lip, divided into two lobes and decorated with a fringe of whiskers, the only hair to be seen on its entire body. Early explorers, for some inexplicable reason, said this creature reminded them of a mermaid but no one in recent times has been able to see the resemblance.

When Europeans arrived on this continent, the manatee was relatively common along the Gulf coast, through the West Indies, and around northern South America. A few individuals wintered as far north as Virginia.

The manatee was hunted for its flesh, oil and skin. It has also been shot for no reason but target practice. Modern motor boats sometimes hit the shallow-swimming manatee and the propellers slash its flesh. In addition, the manatee has suffered from siltation and other pollution of the coastal waters where its feed-

Above: The strangely built manatee.
Opposite: Dappled sunlight filters through the murky depths as the manatee glides silently past.
Below: A manatee swims above a school of fish.

ing grounds are, and occasionally by especially cold winters. Sharks and crocodiles are sometimes accused of killing manatees.

The numbers of manatees have been so reduced that it is now ranked as a seriously endangered mammal, and the State of Florida and the United States government are working to save it. Its current distribution is spotty and its numbers low. The largest refuge for the manatee remains the Everglades National Park. The animal is seen occasionally throughout the Florida Keys. It is also found in Biscayne Bay, the Miami River and New River and still occurs northward as far as the St Johns River at Jacksonville. There is a population of them at Merritt Island Wildlife Refuge. Manatees in small numbers are residents in the Chassahowitzka National Wildlife Refuge and at the J. N. 'Ding' Darling National Wildlife Refuge.

There is very little known about the natural history of the animal. The manatee by nature is a sluggish and sleepy-looking creature. It can sometimes be spotted, resting momentarily on the bottom of a bay where, through the clear water, it looks like a dark spot on the light sand. Then the spot moves, slowly at first, until the creature surfaces. The nostrils protrude through the surface and the manatee exhales noisily. Manatees surface for oxygen frequently but they are capable of submerging for 15 minutes.

The manatee, which has very little defense against predators, attempts to escape by seeking shelter or moving away from the source of danger. The female gives birth to a single calf per year and the newborn young, perhaps 30 inches long, already knows how to swim. When nursing her young one, the female must clasp it to her breast, holding it with her flippers.

The food of the manatee is aquatic vegetation and it eats plants in such quantities that it is frequently suggested as the best answer to the long-time problem of keeping harbors and boat channels open to traffic. The task of clearing away the aquatic weeds, however, is too much to ask of an animal so limited in numbers.

River Otter

Of all the land mammals, the otter is the champion swimmer, a sleek and silent shadow beneath the rippled surface of lake or river. When not in a hurry, the river otter may tilt down to investigate some hidden rock or log, cruise leisurely on its back, belly or side, then turn and twist in acrobatics unmatched by all but the marine mammals.

When necessary, the otter is capable of remarkable bursts of speed. There has long been a question about the otter's ability to swim faster than fish. The question was answered for one biologist as he watched an otter in a large laboratory tank with a school of trout. On the straight-away the otter easily outdistanced the speeding trout. 'I no longer doubt the claim that an otter can outswim a fish,' said the scientist. The otter is believed capable of underwater speeds of six or seven miles an hour.

Games played by otters take many forms. The swimming otter may move along the surface of lake or stream pushing a stick ahead of it with its nose, for no apparent reason. It will sometimes emerge from the depths carrying a clam, then drop its prize, quickly dive and recover it only to drop it and recover it time and again, until it tires of the routine.

Of all the games otters play, they are best known for sliding. In winter, the family group traveling overland across the snow will take full advantage of slopes leading down to open water. The lead animal breaks the trail and others follow. They slide into the water and, apparently enjoying the sport, climb back up the slope and slide down time after time until the hill, wet down by their fur, becomes iced over. Eventually, the dare-devil otters tire of sliding or simply move on in their search for food.

As they travel overland on snow, they employ a brand of half-running, half-sliding that conserves energy while gaining speed. After a short dash they fold their short legs beneath them and slide on their furry bellies reaching speeds of 15 or 20 miles an hour. In summer a mud slide makes a fine substitute for the snow-covered slopes of winter.

Whether otters actually play for the fun of it is something we can not know. But it looks like fun. There can be little doubt, however, that their persistent play serves to sharpen their wits and give them practice in the maneuvering that hunting sometimes demands of them.

Before the arrival on this continent of European people, river otters occupied a remarkably wide range. They lived from Alaska to Labrador and as far south as Florida and the deserts of the Southwest, wherever there was sufficient water to support the foods on which they survived. The arrival of the earliest white settlers was a tragedy for the otters. The animals were shot and trapped for their rich furs. Later the waters where they lived were polluted. Silt, pesticides and wastes from cities and factories reduced populations of aquatic organisms and the creatures dependent on them. Otters vanished from entire regions of the continent. Through much of the United States the otters are now gone. Those remaining are found primarily in 29 states, mostly in the Northwest, Southeast and Northeast and along the upper Great Lakes.

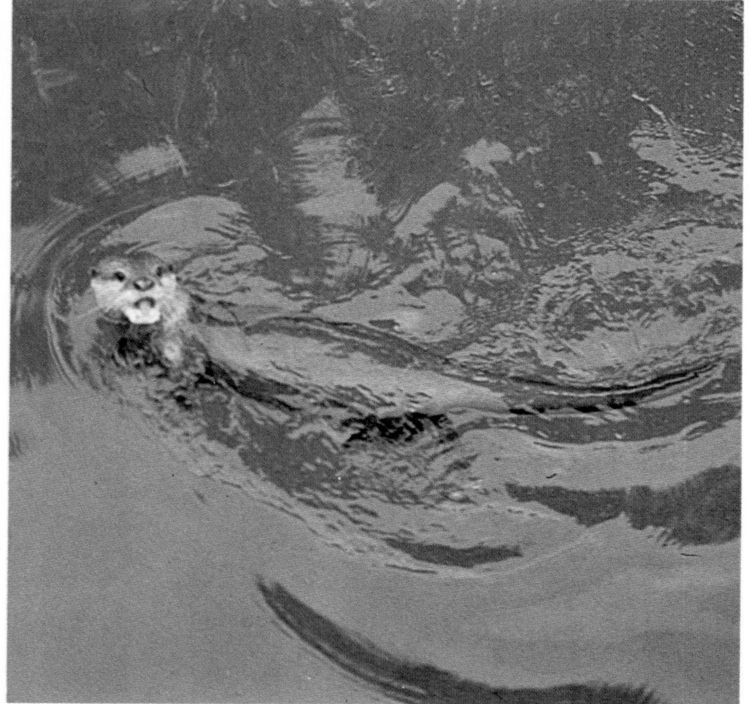

Above: A river otter bares his teeth.
Opposite: A California sea otter floating on his back.

Otters have been vilified for centuries as killers of fish that people wanted. As far back as the fourteenth century, during the reign of Edward II, English gentry pursued the otters with packs of specially-bred otter hounds. The packs were needed for this job because, in the water, the individual dog is no match for an otter.

Biologists have since studied the food habits of river otters with more care. Trappers supplied them stomachs for food analysis and these studies proved that the otter, more than being a fish eater pure and simple, is an opportunist who takes what is available and easiest to capture. Crayfish, which is a favorite, frogs, insects, sluggish fish of little sport or commercial value were all eaten in much greater quantity than were trout. The biologists could uncover little evidence that otters ever cut heavily into the trout population.

Young river otters are born in spring, ordinarily two or three to the litter, but sometimes more. They enter this world in the darkness of a burrow close by the water's edge. They are blind and helpless for six weeks and while they are very young, the male is an outcast not permitted to stay with the family group. But in time, the father returns and again becomes part of the group as the young are old enough to travel and learn to hunt.

When female otters are two years old they reach breeding age and thereafter produce a litter of young each year. And soon these youngsters are swimming and diving, sliding, playing tag and exploring, for this is the life of the otter.

Sea Otter

Sea otters are at home along the western coast of the continent, where they harvest clams, crabs, snails, sea urchins and small fish from shallow saltwater bays.

As the otter surfaces, it may carry, clasped to its breast, one of these treasures. It flips over onto its back and floats, preparing to eat. It may open the shellfish with its paws or teeth, but failing this, it will use its Stone Age tools. The sea otter's tools are rocks brought up from the ocean bottom. Lying on its back with a flat rock resting on its chest, the otter grasps the shellfish in its paws and bangs it down on the rock repeatedly until the shell cracks. Then the meat can be extracted. Advanced otters even use two rocks, one on which to lay the shellfish, the other to crack it.

These sleek sea-going mammals are large members of the weasel clan. The sea otter has a slender body and a broad head with small ears. The legs are short and so is the tail. The hind feet are webbed and this is an aid in swimming. The adult sea otter is four to five feet long, stands only ten or twelve inches high at the shoulders and may weigh 80 pounds or more.

This mammal wears one of the finest of all fur coats, unbelievably soft and extremely dense, a barrier against the cold sea water because the hair locks in a blanket of insulating air.

Although this highly efficient fur has protected the otter from the elements, it has also placed the animal in great jeopardy. The sea otters have been killed for their fur since they were first discovered by Europeans in 1741, when the Russian Czar sent Commander Vitus Bering sailing across the north Pacific on a trip of exploration. This historic trip introduced the world to the beautiful fur of the sea otter. Other ships soon came and the sea otters were under siege. The Russians cleaned out the furs along the Aleutian Islands in Alaska, then moved down the Pacific coast all the way to California.

Many believed that sea otters were extinct and this may have been partly responsible for the fact that the Russians sold Alaska to the United States for two cents an acre in 1867. Then in 1913, when only small groups of otters survived in remote and hidden pockets of the Aleutian Islands, the United States created the Aleutian Islands National Wildlife Refuge and brought full protection to the remaining otters. Gradually, the animals began to increase in remote bays and today they survive in good numbers around Amchitka and other islands in the Aleutians.

The southern sea otters along the California coast, however, are much fewer in numbers and are threatened with extinction.

Sea otters do not rebuild their numbers rapidly; the female produces only one young otter every second year. She is a devoted mother and seldom leaves her youngster unless she must park it temporarily on the surface while she dives for food. Quite often, she takes a firm grip on the baby and carries it along on her under water hunting expeditions.

Sea otters were among the first to discover water beds. They sleep on their backs, drifting on the surface of the bays where they live and, to keep winds and waves from carrying them out to sea while they sleep, they anchor themselves in place with a strip of kelp stretched across their chests. While they try to rest, the pesky gulls may harass them and the otters, in return, splash the gulls with saltwater.

In addition to people, sea otters sometimes face other enemies. The killer whale takes sea otters, and otters may occasionally perish in storms.

Muskrat

This semi-aquatic animal is one of the most common wetland mammals on this continent, ranging from northern Mexico to northern Alaska and Canada. Each year, in Louisiana alone, trappers send nearly a million muskrat furs to market

The furs are used almost exclusively for ladies' coats. In addition, the flesh of the muskrat is eaten by people in some regions where it is commonly called 'marsh hare'. while the musk, which is carried by both male and female muskrats, is used in the perfume industry.

Muskrats cause damage by tunneling into dams and levees, sometimes destroying farm ponds. The major defense against this damage is trapping.

The adult muskrat is covered with a high-quality, brown fur with good wearing qualities, and both sexes look alike. The dense fur of the muskrat protects it from the chilling water in which it spends much of its life. The adult weighs from 1½ to 4 pounds and measures up to 22 inches long. Nearly one-half of the length is tail.

The muskrat's front legs are short, while the hind legs are longer and the feet larger and partly webbed. The animal has small eyes and tiny ears almost hidden in its fur.

Water is the muskrat's refuge. Here the animal is safest. It swims at two to three miles an hour, using its hind feet and tail. It comes out to feed primarily at night and spends much of the daylight hours in its shelter. The muskrat lives in either of two kinds of homes. Some dig burrows into the banks of lakes and streams, others build mound-like houses in the marshes. These muskrat houses, built of cattails and other vegetation, are usually three feet high and four or five feet in diameter at the base. The entrance is commonly underwater, and the home is equipped with a plunge hole and escape runs to be used in times of danger.

Before her young are born, the female muskrat usually gives her home some added touches, plastering the mound with mud from the marsh. The house demands frequent repairs as long as it is used. The young muskrats, as well as the adults, work on the upkeep.

The female gives birth to her young 28 days after breeding. The litter usually contains three to seven 'kits' and at first these infants are blind, nearly helpless and almost naked. The female, however, must leave them when she goes to feed, but she first tucks them into a ball of finely shredded dry grass for comfort.

During the period of nursing, the male has his own quarters in another section of the house, but by the time the young are a week old the female may breed again. Muskrats will normally have two to three litters annually, through much of their range, but in the South may give birth to half a dozen litters.

The young are weaned by the time they are three or four weeks old. Usually the young will not breed until they are about a year old. As they grow to sexual maturity, the young muskrats are driven from the home to spread out over the marsh and establish territories of their own. In this way the colonies may continue to expand until the muskrats crowd each other and fight over available food.

What they eat depends largely on what they can find. Cattails are a common muskrat food. So are roots and stems of three-square bullrush, and other aquatic plants. Muskrats have adapted to eating the farmer's clover, corn and bluegrass when they are accessible. A small part of their diet may be animal matter—crayfish, crabs and even small fish.

Because muskrats are prolific, they make rapid inroads on the food supply and this becomes a factor in population fluctuations. Drought is an enemy of muskrats. So are hurricanes, floods and pollution.

Other enemies stalk the marshes. The lightning-quick mink which, like the muskrat, lives near water, can break into the muskrat's house or enter through the resident's tunnels and if it finds the young there while the parents are off feeding, the losses are heavy. Mink also kill adult muskrats. Other predators, especially on the young, include raccoons, owls, snakes, hawks, fish, turtles, hogs, pet cats and dogs, bullfrogs and, in the South, alligators.

In addition, muskrats are subject to various diseases and the attacks of parasites. All of these forces together take a heavy toll of muskrats and hold the population down.

Opposite: Muskrats, such as this one on the ice in the Tule Lake National Wildlife Refuge in California, are abundant in marshes, ponds and rivers throughout North America. In winter, overpopulation often occurs, resulting in some muskrats being forced to find new homes.

INDEX

ACKNOWLEDGEMENTS

The author and publisher would like to thank the following people who have helped in the preparation of this book: Bill Yenne, who designed it; Thomas G Aylesworth, who edited it.

PHOTO SOURCES

N. P. Baldocchino, USFWS: 109 (upper right).
Robert Belous, NPS: 22 (middle).
Tupper Ansel Blake: 42-43, 50-51, 54-55, 58-59, 63, 159.
Jack Boucher, NPS: 92 (left)
Dick Frear, NPS: 45, 47, 52, 57, 89 (right), 118, 119, 122, 142-143, 148-149, 152 (both), p. 153.
George Harrison, USFWS: 73.
Jerry Hont, USFWS: 14 (bottom).
Don Hultman, USFWS: 102 (top).
J. C. Jones, USFWS: 86.
Elizabeth Joy, NPS: 91.
Joe Keller: 15 (bottom).
William Keller, NPS: 34, 35 (bottom left), 44 top, 79.
Cal Lensink, USFWS: 14 (top).
Jim Leupold, USFWS: 157.
Wayne Lynch, Parks Canada: 3, 67, 74-75, 82, 84-85, 88-89, 94-95, 110, 121.
Jeff Myers: 40-41, 60-61.
Tom Myers: 16, 72.
Keith Mouhouse, USFWS: 17.
National Park Service: 9, 12, 13 (all), 19, 21 (top), 22 (top), 22 (bottom), 36 (top), 36 (bottom left), 38 (top), 44 (bottom), 50, 62, 71 (top), 92 (right), 101 (lower left), 123 (middle), 123 (bottom), 140 (both), 145, 148 (bottom).
David Olson, USFWS: 10, 11 (both).
Danny On, Glacier Natural History Assn.: 20, 21 (bottom), 25, 26-27, 32 (bottom), 48, 53, 56, 65, 136-137.
D. U. Pfitzer, USFWS: 28 (top).
James Powell, USFWS: 154.
Edwin Rothfuss: 4-5.
John Sarvis, USFWS: 18.
Max H. Schroeder: 74 (bottom left).
Richard Simms, Tennessee Wildlife Resources Agency: 2, 8, 90, 93 (bottom), 96, 101 (top), 101 (lower right), 106-107, 111, 112, 113 (top), 113 (bottom), 114-115, 115 (bottom), 116-117, 139, 156, back cover.
Bob Stevens, USFWS: 23 (top).
Cecil Stoughton, NPS: 37 (both), 68-69.
© Glenn R. Steiner, 125, 134, 138-139, 144, 146-147, 150-151.
Hans Stewart, USFWS: 76 (bottom).
Douglas Storer: 87 (both), 130-131, 132-133.
Tennessee Wildlife Resources Agency: 29 (bottom left), 30-31, 32 (top), 33, 102 (bottom), 103, 120, 124, 126-127, 128-129.
USFWS: 28 (bottom), 155 both.
Utah Division of Wildlife Resources: 31 (bottom), 39, 77, 78 (top), 83 (bottom), 93 (top), 97, 123 (top), 135, 29 (top and bottom right), 36 (bottom), 38 (bottom right).
H. Warren, NPS: 22 (bottom), 27 (right).
M. Wick, NPS: 141.
© Bill Yenne: 1, 24, 35 (top), 35 (bottom right), 46, 49, 66, 69 (bottom), 70-71, 71 (bottom), 80, 81, 98, 99, 100, 104, 105, 108, 109 (left), 109 (lower right), Front cover.